Mathematics

Levels 1 - 3

TEACHER'S HANDBOOK

Shirley Clarke

Hodder & Stoughton

LONDON SYDNEY AUCKLAND

Acknowledgments

The author would like to thank all the teachers and children who took part in trialling the assessment activities. Special thanks are due to Jenny Mitchell, who coordinated all the trialling and provided feedback which brings authenticity to the 'What might happen' sections.

The Statements of Attainment cited in this publication are reproduced from *Mathematics in the National Curriculum (1991)*, Department of Education and Science and the Welsh Office, published by Her Majesty's Stationery Office: Crown copyright reserved.

British Library Cataloguing in Publication Data
Clarke, Shirley
    Mathematics. – Levels 1–3. – (Formative
    Assessment in the National Curriculum
    Series)
    I. Title II. Series
    372.7

ISBN 0 340 55773 7

First published 1992

Typeset by Multiplex Techniques Ltd, Orpington.
Printed in Great Britain for the educational publishing division of Hodder & Stoughton Ltd, Mill Road, Dunton Green, Sevenoaks, Kent, by Page Brothers Ltd, Norwich.

Contents

Introduction

This book is a collection of assessment ideas and activities which are related directly to the National Curriculum Mathematics Programmes of Study statements and their corresponding Statements of Attainment (SoAs), for levels 1 to 3. The book has many purposes and can be used in a number of ways.

The assessment activities are *not* intended to represent a scheme in which every child works through every activity. Rather, they can be used:

● as a 'dip-in' collection when you want more information about one child's understanding of one SoA, or about the meaning of the SoA itself;

● when you have 'gaps' in your mathematics records because certain areas of the curriculum have not been covered by a child;

● when a new child arrives in the class and there is a need for some instant assessment;

● to confirm your perceptions about a child's understanding;

● to give you new ideas about the teaching and assessment of the mathematics Attainment Targets, and of the wider scope of mathematics achievement.

Each assessment activity is either (*a*) an activity which needs to be set up; or (*b*) an incidental activity, where assessment is made during a mathematics task (eg sorting) which you would be likely to have happening in the classroom. Most fall into the latter category.

Where an activity needs to be specially set up, game sheets, worksheets or teacher sheets are provided as photocopy masters. Any other resources needed are limited to those which are commonly found in primary classrooms.

The Assessment Activity format

The Statement of Attainment (SoA) is the first point of reference. The related Programmes of Study (PoS) statements are set out underneath the SoA. There then follows a description of the statements – '**About the SoAs and related PoS statements**' – clarifying their meaning, highlighting their most important elements, and showing the relationship between the SoA and the PoS statement(s).

SoAs and PoS statements are often divided into 'attributes' or parts, in which different concepts are referred to, eg '*counting, reading, writing and ordering numbers to at least 10*'. The attributes of this statement are *counting, reading, writing* and *ordering*, so all four need to be dealt with, in both teaching and assessment. References are made to the separate attributes of the statements wherever appropriate throughout this book.

A section on '**Assessment in action**' follows. Instructions are given so that assessment can be made, usually of one or two children. Resources requirements are then listed, and any specific organisational points made.

'**What might happen**' and '**What this tells you**' is shown in a chart. The 'What might happen' section is a list of possible outcomes, all derived from the trialling of the activities (see below). The 'What this tells you' section gives advice as to the level of achievement for each outcome, both in terms of the PoS statement and achievement outside the National Curriculum requirements (eg process and social skills).

The activity concludes with a section entitled '**Developing and extending understanding**'. This lists other mathematical starting points or activities which will help develop concepts or extend children who have achieved the statement. Advice is also given about process, classroom organisation, and on occasions about how children best learn certain mathematical skills or concepts.

The various elements of the activities can of course be used separately, as follows:

● The comments 'About the SoAs and related PoS statements' provide clear interpretation of the statements, which should help demystify the Attainment Targets and enable you to be clearer about teaching aims.

● The 'Developing and extending understanding' section provides suggestions of mathematical starting points, and useful references to good mathematics resource materials, which will enhance your mathematics teaching.

Is there anything else I should know?

The activities, first and foremost, are linked to the National Curriculum Statements of Attainment. This means that a minimal achievement is required to be able to say a child has achieved the SoA. This kind of assessment is called *criterion-referencing*: where a child's performance is measured against a specific statement. Criterion-referencing has only two outcomes: can do or cannot do; in other words, has achieved or has not achieved.

Because criterion-referencing provides only summative, yes/no information, the activities also aim to provide more diagnostic information. This has been facilitated by the range of different outcomes you might expect to happen, based on the trialling of the activities.

For this purpose, the activities were trialled extensively by teachers of different age-groups. A Level 2 activity, for instance, was trialled by a teacher of seven-year-olds, a teacher of five-year-olds and a teacher of nine-year-olds. The children involved were above-average five-year-olds, average seven-year-olds or below-average nine-year-olds, so that the trialling produced a full range of outcomes for the 'What might happen' column.

Trialling teachers felt that there was sometimes a need to be flexible about the activities. Although guidelines have been given, generally common sense will tell you where you should change the instructions to best encourage the child to demonstrate what he or she can do. For example, one child was reluctant to find different ways of making ten. She asked the teacher if she could make eleven instead. The teacher, of course, said this was fine, and the child then engaged in the activity enthusiastically and achieved the SoA, demonstrating a range of problem-solving skills as well. This story has an important message for all aspects of assessment: the context may not suit the child, or the child may need to feel more sense of purpose or control over the activity. It is stated many times throughout the activities that ongoing assessment can only be really reliable if it is based on a number of different assessments in different contexts. However, the National Curriculum poses a huge organisational challenge, in terms of both planning and assessment, so these activities are designed to give as much information as possible from each assessment opportunity.

How many PoS statements need to be achieved for a child to 'pass' the SoA? Do all the SoAs in a level have to be achieved for the child to be awarded that level?
This is completely up to you. The SEAC Key Stage 1 *School Assessment Folder* gives the following advice:

'When you come to decide which level on each attainment target to allocate to a child, you will need to consider whether the child has achieved the statements of attainment given at that particular level. Different attainment targets can be treated in different ways.
   'For some attainment targets you may put together your separate judgements for each statement. This may be the best approach in those containing unrelated aspects of knowledge. For other attainment targets your assessment could be a single overall judgement which takes account of all the statements of attainment.'

In other words, you can decide for yourself what constitutes a child achieving a level, as long as you 'consider' the statements of attainment. You may decide that achievement of half or more of the SoAs in a level is enough for a child to be awarded that level. Alternatively, you may decide on 100% achievement, or even an overall 'feeling' of whether a child is at that level or not. SEAC clearly leaves this very important decision in the hands of the professionals, who, after all, know the children's abilities better than anyone else. It will obviously be better if a policy about this is agreed in your school, so that there is consistency and continuity, for both teachers and children.

For further ideas

The following books and other resources are mentioned in the text or would be useful:

BEAM packs: *Odds and Evens, Hollows and Solids, Triangles and Quadrangles, Early Levels Packs 1 and 2, What's the Chance?, Growth, Spot the Pattern,* also *Starting from Scratch, Starting from Pegboards, Starting from Geoboards, Starting from Number Lines* and *Starting from Squared Paper* (available from BEAM Project, Block C, Barnsbury Complex, Offord Road, London N1).

The Book of Think and *The I Hate Mathematics! book* by Marilyn Burns (Little, Brown and Company).

Bounce To It!: A collection of investigations and problems for infants, by G. Hatch, G. Marriott and J. Savin (Manchester Polytechnic).

Bright Ideas: Maths Games (Scholastic).

Cambridge Primary Mathematics scheme games.

Children and Number: difficulties in learning mathematics, by Martin Hughes (Basil Blackwell).

Count Me In games (Harcourt Brace Jovanovitch).

I don't know: Let's find out: Mathematical Investigations in the Primary School, by W. Garrard (Mathematical Association).

'Magic Mirror' books (eg *Another, Another, Another and More; Annette; Make a bigger puddle, make a smaller worm*), by Marion Walter (Andre Deutsch)

Mathematics Their Way and *Workjobs,* by Mary Baratta-Lorton (Addison-Wesley).

Mathematics with Reason, by Sue Atkinson (Hodder & Stoughton).

Mathematics with seven and eight year olds, by Marion Bird (Mathematical Association).

Nelson Mathematics scheme games.

Nuffield *Bronto* books (Longman).

Nuffield Mathematics: Teachers Handbooks 1 and 2 (Longman).

Piers is Lost...and other school-based real problem solving activities (resources for Learning Development Unit, Avon).

What's in the Square? (Arnold).

Legodacta

Computer software: *Grass* (Neumann Software, Neumanns College); *Ourfacts* (National Council for Educational Technology); *Clipboard* (Blackcats).

Robots: *Pip* (Swallow Systems) and *Roamer* (Valiant Technology).

Ma 1

Ma 1/1a Use mathematics as an integral part of practical classroom tasks.
Ma 1/2a Select the materials and the mathematics to use for a practical task.
Ma 1/3a Find ways of overcoming difficulties when solving problems.

Related PoS statements
- Using materials for a practical task. (PoS 1/1a)
- Selecting the materials and the mathematics to use for a practical task. (PoS 1/2a)
- Selecting the materials and the mathematics to use for a task using alternative approaches to overcome difficulties. (PoS 1/3a)

About the SoAs and related PoS statements

Level 1

These statements require a child to become involved in a practical task, using materials which may have been provided or selected. The child should also use mathematics in some form, either as instructed by the teacher or as chosen by the child. The SoA focuses on the *process* of the task: 'getting it right' is not essential.

Level 2

'Select the materials' implies that there must be a range of accessible maths equipment from which the child is free to select.
    Giving a child a context in which he or she has an opportunity to demonstrate his/her ability to 'select the mathematics' is more difficult, as the context of a problem often dictates the mathematics which needs to be used. For example, a child might be asked 'How many ways can you find to *add* two numbers so that the answer is 10?' In order to assess this part of this statement, therefore, the child should be presented with a more open-ended context in which he/she has to decide how to go about solving the problem.
    As with Level 1, there is no requirement for the child to arrive at the *correct* answer.

Level 3

Children often get 'stuck' when solving a problem. This SoA focuses on their ability to think of another way of solving the problem. This may mean using different resources or a different method. It will be easier for children to achieve this if they have been encouraged by a teacher to solve problems by using their own (often original) methods, and if they feel that different methods for solving the same problem are valued.

Assessment in action

Level 1

Observe the child involved in any of the following, or similar experiences:

- sharing out paper, pencils, scissors, etc;
- counting money, children in a group, how many of anything is needed, etc;
- finding out some aspect of measure (eg the height/weight/length of something) using any method;

– matching cups to saucers, pictures, etc, in real or constructed situations;
– sequencing picture cards or events orally;
– using construction toys or apparatus (eg Lego, Duplo) and talking about this.

Level 2

Observe the child involved in a 'finding out' situation, which is of a mathematical nature, such as:

How many times can you write your name in a minute?
Who has the longest arms in the group/class, etc?
Find out how much it will cost to buy three packets of biscuits for our outing.
Find out how many pencils we need if everybody has two.
Find out which of the different shaped containers will hold the most cubes.
Find out how long it takes us to walk to assembly.

Level 3

In any of the above Level 2 situations, or similar, make sure you ask the child to discuss his/her work with you at regular intervals (eg 'How are you going to do it?...Try it out, then come and tell me what happened...'). This will enable you to have a dialogue about difficulties which arise.

What might happen	*What this tells you*
Level 1	
1 Shows evidence of any of the following: counting, attempting to measure, matching, sequencing, using comparative or positional language (eg 'taller', 'bigger', 'under', etc) or any other mathematical skill.	*The child achieves the statement.* Level 1 is looking for early mathematical knowledge which is largely instinctive at this stage. It is important that the child is attempting to *use* mathematics: correctness is not necessary.
2 Is able to use 'mathematics' in limited areas only (eg counting but not comparative language).	Children's early maths ability is bound up with language development and context. You will have to decide how much evidence constitutes 'using maths as an integral part'.
Level 2	
1 Decides on a way of solving the problem and uses anything available to carry it out.	*Achieves the statement.* The statement is not asking for advanced mathematics, but simply that the child can decide on a method and use whatever is appropriate to solve the problem. The method and materials are likely to be invented, and not necessarily conventional or correct. (See below for a list of observable features when children are problem-solving.)
2 Tries to solve the problem inappropriately and gives a 'silly' answer.	The answer does not have to be correct, but you will need to decide whether the child has been engaged in a mathematical *process* (eg trying to count/time something). You could ask the child to guess/predict the answer beforehand to find out more about the child's perception and understanding of the task (eg if the child says '5p' for the three packets of biscuits, you know something about the child's experience of number/ shopping/quantity, etc).

What might happen (cont)	*What this tells you*
3 Does not engage in the task.	The child probably needs exploratory play situations, in order to identifiy properties of shape, size and quantity and acquire the associated language, before going on to find out specifics.

Level 3

1 Is able to either think of another method or adapt the situation to help solve the problem (eg try using a different resource or rebuild something).	*Achieves the statement.* The child does not have to solve the problem, but be able to cope with difficulties. Collaborative problem-solving is more likely to lead to varied strategies than individual work. Use this opportunity to identify other problem-solving skills the children might be using (see list below).
2 Gives logical but non-mathematical suggestions for overcoming difficulties (eg says 'let's use the pencils we've already got').	This should be viewed as evidence of mathematical thinking; using lateral, strategic thinking and relying on common sense. Children often give such answers in order to achieve success when they know they can't do what is really expected. Use this opportunity to give supportive suggestions (eg 'Would it help if...? Have you tried...? Let's see if we can do it together...', etc). Collaborative problem-solving and whole-class feedback are probably the best ways of developing children's problem-solving strategies.
3 Gives up when difficulties arise.	Needs non-threatening collaborative problem-solving situations and more experience of a range of problems. It is often important to help a child to achieve success by giving constructive advice and suggestions, then give praise for the child's achievements. When children lack confidence it can be difficult to stop this permeating all maths work, so you need to build it at all opportunities. It is also important to point out difficulties in whole-class sharing times, confronting them and showing how much you learn from finding something does *not* work.

Developing and extending understanding

- Even from Reception age, there should be a table or area for maths equipment, which is accessible to the children. It should include:
  - calculators;
  - number lines (0–100);
  - counting objects such as cubes/bottle tops/counters;
  - multi-base equipment (eg Dienes);
  - measuring devices (tape measures, rulers, surveyors' tapes, stop watch, clock, different types of weighing devices, lengths of string, etc);
  - 2-D and 3-D shapes, Logiblocs;
  - different types of dice (size, shape, numbers).

Try labelling containers of these resources, or drawing round the bottoms of the containers, so that children can tidy up easily.

If children are encouraged to handle, play with and experiment with the resources, they will become confident in including them in their maths work. This area can also include an 'investigation-of-the-week card' and other interesting mathematical games or puzzles to attract children to it.

- Different sizes, thicknesses and types of paper should also be easily accessible to children, including scrap paper (best in the centre of each table in the classroom) for 'having a go' at maths (and English), without feeling that it should be first-time perfect.

- If children are encouraged to use the resources to find out how to solve a problem (even sums), they will find their own methods of working things out. These may not be the most efficient, but it is important that children first establish an understanding of maths and 'take ownership' of it. Once children are confident with their own methods, they can be shown standard notation and traditional conventions.

Things you may observe while children are involved in problem-solving and investigations
(*not in any order, and not exhaustive*)

- can collaborate with others
- can share space and materials
- can discuss work with other children or teachers
- can work independently
- can organise themselves
- is able to help someone else
- can listen to another child or the teacher
- can explain what they are doing or have done
- asks questions
- attitude:
  enthusiastic
  persistent
  gives up easily
  confident
  interested
  aware of new things and ideas
- can choose and find appropriate equipment and materials

- can make sensible predictions
- can estimate
- can work systematically
- can develop strategies for overcoming problems
- can use previous experience to help solve a problem
- can analyse the result and is able to make appropriate changes
- has own ideas (doesn't need to be told what to do)
- can make decisions
- is able to make observations and record
- is able to ask for help when needed
- can collect and organise information
- can hypothesise
- can extend the problem
- is willing to experiment and take risks
- has good manipulative skills
- has good spacial awareness

Ma 1

Ma 1/1b Talk about their own work and respond to questions.

Ma 1/2b Talk about work or ask questions using appropriate mathematical language.

Ma 1/3b Use or interpret appropriate mathematical terms and mathematical aspects of everyday language in a precise way.

Ma 1/3c Present results in a clear and organised way.

Related PoS statements
- Talking about their work and asking questions. (PoS 1/1b)
- Describing work and checking results. (PoS 1/2b)
- Explaining work and recording findings systematically. (PoS 1/3b)

About the SoAs and related PoS statements

Level 1

These statements are essentially attitudinal in nature, referring to a child developing an interested and enquiring mind, and one assessment opportunity will not necessarily demonstrate a child's attitude to something. Although an activity is outlined here, there will be many more opportunities in the course of the mathematics a child encounters, where evidence of developing curiosity about mathematics will present itself.

'Respond to questions' does not necessarily imply that the responses need to be correct, but rather that the child should make a response which is appropriate to the question.

The 'asking questions' attribute in the PoS statement poses problems for assessment, as children at this stage are unlikely to ask a question about their work, but will show evidence of a questioning mind in other ways. Skilful questioning by the teacher, however, can encourage a child to show a questioning attitude (eg 'What else could you try to find out?' is likely to produce a response in which the child gives an idea for investigating).

Level 2

'Using appropriate mathematical terms' refers to the use of any mathematical language in the correct context (eg *add, subtract, triangle, sides, taller*, etc).

In the PoS statement, 'describing' does not have to be oral, but can be in a written form. 'Checking results' implies that another method should be used, if appropriate, to validate the child's first solution (this could be with a calculator). Although the spirit of the PoS statement seems to imply that the child should check his/her results as a matter of course, for assessment purposes he/she could be *asked* to check and the assessment could focus on the use of a different method, if appropriate.

Level 3

Ma 1/3b refers to the use of correct terminology in the context of a description (eg 'I added the tens together first, then divided by three' rather than 'I put those numbers all in, then I shared them into three', or similar).

'Interpret appropriate mathematical terms ...' refers to the child's understanding of terms used by other people or in problems themselves. This could be assessed by listening to children talking about a problem, or in the course of your discussions about a problem with a child.

'Explaining', in the PoS statement, suggests that the child should be able to give a coherent account of the processes he/she has used, so that someone else can understand what has been done. The ability to 'record findings systematically' is an important stage in children's mathematical perceptions, as this shows that they are beginning to organise and make sense of the elements of a problem. Any *ordering* of data indicates a systematic approach.

Assessment in action

Use the assessment activity on page 62 (PoS 3/2a) as a starting point.

PoS 1/1b, 2b, 3b

Ask the child to tell you what he/she has done, and encourage talk about the counters/cubes.

A reliable assessment can only be made over a period of time, however, based on a child's general attitude to maths.

PoS 1/3c

Ask the child to record the different ways to make 8 as clearly as possible, so that you can easily see whether any combinations have been missed out.

At the end, talk to the child about his/her work.

What might happen	*What this tells you*
Level 1b	
1 Talks about the task (eg 'I made three numbers', 'I've got three red ones and five blue ones') in response to your questions.	*Achieves the statement.* You may not need to ask the questions if you notice the child responding to another child's questions, as this will still indicate achievement.
2 Engages in the task, but does not communicate with other children, or you, about it.	Needs individual encouragement and attention. Ask questions which are easy to answer, to encourage talk.
3 Talks about the task, but only makes the number in one way.	Make sure the child has understood the task. Although there is no evidence of mathematical curiosity for this task, it may be because the child is not motivated by this context. Form your opinion of whether the child has attained the statement by responses to questions, rather than ability to succeed at the task.
Level 2b/3b	
1 Tells you about the task, using appropriate mathematical terms (eg *three/numbers/ four/add*, etc).	*Achieves the level 2b statement.* Some of the child's talk may be inaccurate or imprecise mathematically, but he/she obviously knows appropriate terms as single words.

What might happen (cont)	*What this tells you*
2 Tells you about the task in a precise, descriptive style, which is mathematically correct (eg 'I found six ways of making 8: 2 plus 6, 3 plus 5 ...', etc), *or* clearly understands your correct use of maths terminology by the responses offered.	*Achieves the level 3b statement.* The difference between levels 2 and 3 is the ability to describe in or interpret mathematically precise sentences. If other children are involved in this task, use a sharing time to allow children to show each other the different ways they have recorded the results.

Level 3c

1 Explains the work done in a coherent way (eg 'I've made 8 in six ways, first I ...') and records the numbers systematically, eg $1 + 7, 2 + 6, 3 + 5$ *or* ● ○ ○ ○ ○ ○ ○ ○ 　　● ● ○ ○ ○ ○ ○ ○ 　　● ● ● ○ ○ ○ ○ ○ *or* 8 + 0　　　　3 + 5 　　0 + 8　　　　5 + 3	*Achieves the statement* if the work is recorded systematically, even if the work is not explained well.
2 Explains coherently, but does not record systematically.	Needs 'combinations' problem-solving practice (see extension ideas for PoS 3/2a). Help the child to organise data from these problems, eg 'Using red and green, how many different ways can you colour this flag?': 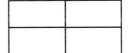 'Let's start with one red and three greens. Where shall we start with the red?' 　'Now where could the red go in the next flag?'
3 Cannot record findings systematically.	Make sure the child understood the task. Try other 'combinations' problems to see whether the context did not inspire the child.

Developing and extending understanding

- Children could be given mathematical starting points to work on in pairs or groups, so that talking about the maths becomes natural to them.

- Sharing sessions, in which children show their work, can be used to build confidence about children's own method of recording.

- See also the extension ideas for PoS 3/2a.

Ma 1

Ma 1/1c   Make predictions based on experience.
Ma 1/2c   Respond appropriately to the question: 'What would happen if …?'
Ma 1/3d   Investigate general statements by trying out some examples.

Related PoS statements
- Making predictions based on experience (PoS 1/1c)
- Asking and responding to questions, eg 'What would happen if …?', 'Why …?'. (PoS 1/2c)
- Investigating and testing predictions and general statements. (PoS 1/3c)
- Checking results, considering whether they are sensible. (PoS 1/3d)

About the SoA and related PoS statements

Level 1

The statements specifically require that the predictions should be 'based on experience'. To give the child the best opportunity to succeed, assessment of this SoA should closely follow the related experience. The assessment here reflects this. The *process* of making a prediction, rather than the accuracy of the prediction itself, is the criterion for success.

Level 2

'What would happen if …?' is the kind of question one child might ask another when they are engaged in a practical investigation, perhaps suggesting a change in the 'rules' they are applying (eg after playing a game with a die, he/she might ask 'What would happen if we used two dice?').

Children often find it easier to respond to questions than to formulate them themselves, although a child's behaviour can sometimes demonstrate that he/she is posing the question to him/herself (eg after exploring the possible number of different arrangements of three cubes, he/she spontaneously goes on to explore the possibilities with four).

Level 3

PoS 1/3c refers to the kind of general statement which is often used as a starting-point investigation (eg an even + an odd number is always odd/7 is the most likely total when rolling two dice – investigate). By investigating, or trying out some examples, children would then be achieving this statement.

Ways in which children might check results to see whether they are sensible, as required by **PoS 1/3d**, are:

- using the same method again to check for possible errors
- using a different method or different resources

It is important that children are asked 'How do you know it's right/true?' when they tell you they have solved a problem. This will mean they have to explain to you *how* they know, or admit that they are not sure, and will need to try another method to be certain.

Assessment in action

Use the assessment activity on page 24 (PoS 2/2a) and Resource Sheet 2 as a starting point.

Level 1

After the game has been played, ask the child how the game would be different if you put lots more numbers on the cat.

Level 2

If the child answers correctly (see 'What might happen'), say '*What would happen in the game if you could only* **add** *the numbers on the dice?*'

Level 3

Give the child the two dice and ask if it is true that 7 is the total you most often get if you roll two dice lots of times. Encourage the child to try it out, to see (**PoS 1/3c**).

After the child has given an answer, ask 'How do you know if you are right?, How could you check what you've done, to be absolutely sure?' (**PoS 1/3d**). (It is not essential to achieve this PoS statement to achieve the SoA.)

What might happen · *What this tells you*

Level 1

What might happen	*What this tells you*
1 Makes any sensible prediction, eg 'It would take a long time', 'It would be harder/easier', 'The numbers would be squashed', 'You'll need a bigger cat', 'You wouldn't be able to read the numbers'.	*Achieves the statement.* Follow up any ideas if children indicate that they would like to extend the game (eg put more numbers in/use different dice/make up their own rules).
2 Says something which is not a prediction, eg 'I've got a cat', 'You mustn't draw on the cat'.	Try rephrasing the question after talking about the child's cat, for instance, as the child may simply want to talk to you. If he/she does not then make a prediction, he/she needs practical experiences where making a prediction is natural (eg building towers, making cakes, moulding Plasticine, filling containers).

Level 2

1 Says something which relates to the maths, eg 'You wouldn't be able to get some of the numbers', 'You can't get a 1 or a 0 if you don't subtract', 'You would need to take away to get all the numbers', 'You would need a lot of dice', 'You'll need more counters'.	*Achieves the statement.*
2 Says something which shows the child is not relating specifically to the maths, eg 'It would take too long', 'It would be boring'.	Needs more experience of developing maths starting points (eg changing one of the elements of a problem in order to investigate further) or needs further questioning (eg 'Why?').

What might happen (cont)	*What this tells you*
Level 3	
1 Tries rolling the dice and recording the totals in some way, in order to test your theory.	*Achieves the SoA.* Ask if they can tell you why this is, to assess the extent of their understanding.
2 Tells you that the statement is not true, after trying it out.	If the child tells you that the statement is not true, the SoA is still achieved – only trying out examples is required.
3 Tells you that the statement is true, without trying it out.	This shows that the child is either guessing or does actually know it to be true. See if the child can tell you how they know, to find out the extent of their understanding. Either way, you will need to use another general statement to motivate the child to 'try it out' to test the theory.
4 Tries it out, but does not keep a careful enough record to be able to judge the results.	As long as the child engaged in the process correctly, the SoA is achieved. Use this situation as a way of helping the child to be systematic: suggest recording each throw in a list or some kind of frequency table.

Developing and extending understanding

- Any mathematical starting point can be developed in some way, regardless of its content, for example:

  $25 + 12 = 37$ → How many different ways can you make that number?

  → How many different totals can you make by rearranging the three numbers?

  → ... by changing the sign?

  Developments from a starting point lend themselves to predictions. Ask children what they think the answer will be, before they test it out. This gives them a point of reference, enhances motivation and develops mathematical thinking. Eventually, children will begin to make predictions without your asking, and will begin to see how to develop starting points without your intervention.

- Use the Cat Game and the children's ideas which spring from the prediction questions to extend the game, for example:

  - more numbers on the cat,
  - fewer numbers on the cat,
  - different numbers on the cat,
  - different numbers on the die,
  - different rules (adding/subtracting),
  - more dice.

  See also the extension ideas for PoS 2/2a, page 25.

Ma 2/1a Use number in the context of the classroom and school.

Related PoS statements
- Counting, reading, writing and ordering numbers to at least 10. (PoS 2/1a)
- Learning that the size of a set is given by the last number in the count. (PoS 2/1b)
- Understanding the language associated with number, eg 'more', 'fewer', 'the same'. (PoS 2/1c)
- Understanding conservation of number. (PoS 2/1d)
- Making a sensible estimate of a number of objects up to 10. (PoS 2/1e)

About the SoA and related PoS statements

The SoA uses the word 'number', which gives the possibility of any size of number. The clarifying PoS statements use the limit of the number 10 as a minimal requirement only. Young children should be encouraged to explore large numbers, especially in real-life situations (eg door numbers) and in experimentation with calculators ('I can make it go 100, 200, 300 ...').

PoS 2/1a, 1b

These statements contain five separate (although related) attributes, the last one being 'Learning that the size ... count'.

'Writing' implies not only knowing how to write the symbols, but also knowing the connections (eg the word 'six' is written '6' and refers to a quantity of six).

PoS 2/1c

This kind of terminology usually arises when comparing set size. The word 'less' is often wrongly used, as it refers to 'whole masses of quantities': 'fewer' is correct for numerical quantities (eg 'We need less Plasticine', 'We need ten fewer pencils'). Children become familiar with these terms if the teacher uses them in real-life situations.

PoS 2/1d

Conservation is notoriously difficult to assess. The traditional Piagetian test asks children to say whether there is still the same number of objects after they have been rearranged, eg a line of objects being spaced out to look longer. Research shows that children are influenced by the lack of context and that they often say the number has changed because the question implies that it has, and because they like to please the teacher. The related assessment aims at seeing whether a child knows how to conserve number.

PoS 2/1e

This statement has two 'difficult' elements: the word 'sensible' and the worth of estimating such a small number. 'Sensible' suggests a number within two or three of the actual amount. The ability to estimate such a small number of objects is itself difficult to assess, as children can often 'count' the objects in the same time it takes to make an estimate. The related assessment aims to deal with these problems.

PoS 2/1a   **Counting, reading, writing and ordering numbers to at least 10.**

PoS 2/1b   **Learning that the size of a set is given by the last number in the count.**

Assessment in action

Part 1   Observe the child counting ten objects. Choose objects which are easy to count, and a normal classroom context and ask, eg, 'How many pairs of scissors do we have?', 'How many red pencils are left in this box?' (Assesses: *Counting numbers to at least 10; learning that the size of a set is given by the last number in the count.*)

Part 2   Ask the child to cut along the lines of Resource Sheet 1 and **write** on the blank cards, to make a 'set' of one to ten number cards. He/she should then put them in **order** on the desk to check they are all there. (Assesses: *Reading, writing and ordering numbers to at least 10.*)

Cut the cards out for any child who may have difficulty with this. It is important not to alienate the child from the task.

What might happen | What this tells you

Part 1

What might happen	What this tells you
1 Counts accurately with one-to-one correspondence and says the last number again as the total.	*Achieves both attributes.* Try level 2a if you believe the child could count to 100.
2 Makes one slip, therefore making the total inaccurate.	Ask the child to count again, maybe on another occasion. Even adults sometimes miscount at times. Sometimes a slip may occur because the person counting is very competent and counts 'automatically'.
3 Writes some numbers, then doesn't know which numbers are still needed.	Probably knows the numbers, but need help with organising. Help the child check which numbers he/she already has, maybe suggesting he/she writes the numbers 1 to 10 on a piece of paper and checks them off.
4 Says the numbers in order, but does not have one-to-one correspondence (a counting number for each object).	Needs counting rhymes, matching activities and counting by *moving* objects one at a time, rather than by pointing to them.
5 Says numbers at random.	This shows an awareness of the purpose of numbers, but the child has not yet learnt the counting names in order or developed the concept of one-to-one correspondence.
6 Says the wrong number for the total.	This is likely to happen if the child also said the numbers at random or does not have one-to-one correspondence.

What might happen (cont)	*What this tells you*
Part 2	
1 Writes the remaining numbers and orders the cards (from left to right or right to left).	*Achieves the remaining three attributes.*
2 Writes the numbers but some incorrectly, and orders the cards.	Reversals are acceptable, as the child knows the basic shapes of the numbers but has problems with their orientation. *Achieves the three attributes.*
3 Writes some numbers illegibly and cannot order the cards correctly.	Needs skill practice of writing numbers. (Try recording dice-throws with a numeral die, aiming to see which number is rolled the most.)

Developing and extending understanding

- Children need to be immersed in numbers, up to 10 and beyond, in many forms and contexts. Research shows that young children are capable of understanding and handling very large numbers, if they have access to calculators and can record and solve problems in their own way.

- Encourage counting in class situations (eg lining up, how many children in a group?, etc) to help children remember the sequence of the numbers. Counting rhymes and songs are also helpful.

- Children need to begin counting by playing matching one-to-one games (eg who has most conkers? – match one-to-one in a line to see) and comparing sets for more, less or same. Once these concepts are established, counting a set of objects will have significance, in that the total number denotes the *size* of the set.

- When counting objects, encourage children to *move* them as they count, from one side to another, so that one-to-one correspondence is reinforced and there are no miscounts. Many children make 'mistakes' in counting because they forget which objects they have counted, or where they started from.

- Ordering falls into two categories: ordering the number symbols, and ordering sets of objects. Children often find it easier to order numbers if the sequence is well known, than sets of objects, especially if the objects in each set vary in size.

  Help develop ordering skills in real contexts, for example:

  - class surveys can be done physically (in the hall); get into groups of favourite colour, sort out the groups in order of size.
  - count pencils in each groups' pots and put in order, so we can see which tables need new pencils.

  Games such as those in *Count Me In* (HBJ) are also excellent for developing ordering skills.

● The activity can be used to develop the mathematics as follows:

Part 1

Develop the problem, for example:

- 'How many scissors do we need for one between two this morning?'
- 'How many more red pencils shall I get if each table has a new one for their pot?'
- 'How many books will fit in this way?'

Part 2

Use the set of cards to:

- play Snap! with a partner,
- make up a game,
- see how many different totals can be made by adding or subtracting different cards (eg 2 + 3 = 5),
- see how many different numbers can be made by combining the cards (eg 2, 3 and 4 = 234).

PoS 2/1c   **Understanding the language associated with number, eg 'more', 'fewer', 'the same'.**

Assessment in action

This statement lends itself to incidental assessment. Any of the following contexts would be suitable:

- sorting sets of objects;
- discussing how many children are in today;
- giving out scissors, pencils, etc;
- playing a game where players collect counters, cards, etc.

In the course of your usual interaction with the child engaged in the task, talk to him/her, asking questions which use mathematical terms, such as:

- 'Which set has more in it?'
- 'Have any of your sets got the same number of objects?'
- 'How many more children are in today, compared to yesterday?'
- How many would we have if there were two fewer?'
- 'We need more scissors – how many more?'
- 'Who has the same number as me?'

What might happen	*What this tells you*
1 Understands your questions, but does not use the terms in his/her own talk	*Achieves the statement.* 'Understands' is all that is required. It is likely that the child will soon use the terms if understanding of them is clear.
2 Only understands 'more' and 'same', but not 'fewer'.	*Achieves the statement.* The words given are examples only. The child will need to hear unfamiliar words used in real-life contexts.
3 Uses only 'awkward' language and appears not to understand correct terminology.	Children need to express numerical quantity and other characteristics in their own language first. Reinforce the child's own words by repeating them, but also state alternative, correct terms when discussing mathematics (eg 'Yes, your number is bigger than mine – you have more than me').

Developing and extending understanding

- Maths discussion is vital if children are to learn correct terminology (and to become competent problem-solvers).

    Encourage collaborative tasks, in pairs, and provide maths number games (the infants maths games packs published by Cambridge University Press and by Nelson are very good, and *Bright Ideas: Maths Games* (Scholastic) is useful. Games are especially effective in encouraging children to talk about number (eg 'I need 6 more', 'We both got the same number', 'That's too many').

The following list of observation prompts describes some of the different kinds of social, process and maths skills which can be learnt through game-playing:

Things you may observe while children are playing games
(Not in any order, and not exhaustive)

Social skills	Process skills	Maths skills
Contributes verbally during game	Uses counters for operations	Matches colours
Takes turn	Uses fingers for operations	Has 1 – 1 correspondence when counting
Can explain the game to others	Organises playing pieces in an orderly way during game	Recognises dice spots as that number
Can help others in a game	Can invent an extension or new rule	Can match dice spots with numerals
Accepts help in a game	Has strategies for winning	Can sequence size by nesting/by order
Understands fairness	Uses memory as a strategy	Can order numbers
Enjoys game playing	Uses a calculator with confidence	Has linked concrete with symbol – to 6 – to 12
	Predicts the outcome of moves in a game	Has recall of addition number bonds to 12 Has recall of subtraction bonds to 12
	Predicts the outcome of calculator presses	
	Can tell what happened after a game	

PoS 2/1d   **Understanding conservation of number.**

Assessment in action ▨▨▨▨▨▨▨▨▨▨▨▨▨▨▨▨▨▨▨▨▨▨▨▨▨▨▨▨▨

There are a variety of occasions which lend themselves to the assessment of conservation of number. Choose one of these, or a similar situation, in which to assess a child's ability.

- After a child has built a tower of 3-D shapes, ask how many shapes are in the tower. As soon as the child has put them back in the box, ask 'How many shapes did you put back?'

- After first counting how many children are on the carpet, line them up and ask the child 'How many children are lined up?'

- After counting the calculators on the maths resource table, distribute them for a maths session and ask 'How many calculators are there in the classroom?'

    Alternatively, play the following 'game' with a small group of children. It shows their ability to conserve number and colour:

– The children count out a number of cubes (not more than ten, in two or three different colours).
– They cover the cubes with a yoghurt pot/container and shake it up.
– They uncover the cubes.
– They say what is the same about their cubes and what is different.

    In all these activities, it is important that the child should not *expect* a change in the number of 'objects' rearranged (eg don't ask the 'lining up' question if some children have come in late; don't use the 'calculator' question if some children have their own calculators in the classroom).

    Make sure the conservation question is asked very soon after the original number has been counted, or the child might forget the number.

What might happen	*What this tells you*
1 The child says that the number of objects would be the same, or repeats the actual number.	*Achieves the statement.*
2 The child counts the 'objects' again in order to find out, or guesses at a number.	Has not yet grasped that the number of objects stays the same if rearranged. (If you are not sure whether the child recounted in order to check that new objects had not 'appeared', re-assess using a more controlled situation, eg the cubes.)
3 The child counts the objects wrongly in the first instance, but shows an understanding of conservation by repeating that number when asked the question.	The count of objects does not have to be correct for this assessment. *The child is demonstrating achievement of the statement.*

Developing and extending understanding

- Use headless matches, tiles, pieces of pasta, etc, to make different arrangements of a given number (eg 'How many different ways can you arrange three matches?'). This will help children grasp the idea that a number stays the same although it can 'look' different.

- Play a game like 'Statues', where children change their position. If no one is 'out', ask 'How many in the game?' Ask the same question as children go 'out', to develop mental subtraction.

PoS 2/1e

Making a sensible estimate of a number of objects up to 10.

Assessment in action

(This task also forms the starting point of an assessment of Ma 1 at levels 1 and 2.)

Give a pair of children a box containing 7, 8 or 9 large cubes and make a game of the task: *'Guess how many cubes are in the box (whisper the guess to me or write it on a "secret" note), then count them together to find out exactly how many there are.'*

What might happen	*What this tells you*
1 Estimates the number to within two or three of the total amount.	*Achieves the statement.*
2 Estimates the number to within 10, but is more than two or three away from the total.	Needs more experience of using objects for a variety of mathematical tasks, so that the relationship between size and quantity become linked in a meaningful situation.
3 Says a number which is not sensible (eg a million, 56, etc).	Needs experience as above, but also lots of counting activities, where real objects are counted . The child may be totally unmotivated, but trials showed that most children enjoyed this game.

Developing and extending understanding

- Children should be encouraged to make a prediction or estimate of the outcome for all mathematical starting points, for example:

  - How tall do you think it will be?
  - How long do you think it will take?
  - What might happen?

  This gives children a point of reference and comparison as they are working at a problem, and also helps them to focus on looking at solutions in a commonsense way first, rather than seeking a precise answer.

- An estimate should also be used to show a child what he/she has learnt, for example: *'So it was 65 and you thought it would be 10 – so you've learnt that the box holds more than you thought'*

  Develop this whenever possible, for example: *'So how many do you think* **this** *size box will hold?'*

  Applaud the child's new perception and point out how much the child has learnt.

- The game can be extended in the following ways:

  - Try more cubes: how good are you at estimating?
  - Use more cubes and each child takes a handful: guess each other's handful and count afterwards.
  - As above, but see who has the most, either by counting or matching one to one.
  - Use 'target' cards (eg nearest to 10   an even number   nearest to 15). Choose one of the cards, then take a handful of cubes each. Count out handfuls to see who was the 'target' winner. Deciding who is nearest a certain number can bring in all kinds of interesting strategies (eg 'Is 7 or 12 nearest to 10?', 'How can we find out?', 'Use a number line/cubes', 'Write the numbers?', etc).

Ma 2

Ma 2/1b Add and subtract using a small number of objects.

Related PoS statement
- Using addition and subtraction, with numbers no greater than 10, in the context of real objects. (PoS 2/1f)

About the SoA and related PoS statement

The SoA does not define the number of objects, although this is clarified in the PoS. The greatest number *arrived at* should be 10, rather than using numbers up to 10 (eg 6 + 3 but not 9 + 4).

Assessment in action

This statement lends itself to incidental assessment, during the course of normal classroom work, so that the context is meaningful for the child. The following are the kinds of situations which offer opportunity to assess a child's ability to add and subtract using objects:

- Ask a child to bring you, say, three pieces of lined paper and two pieces of plain. Ask *'How many pieces of paper have you brought me altogether?'*

  Give the child one piece of paper back and say *'I've decided I don't need this one. How many pieces of paper have I got now?'*

- Ask a child to make numbers with some red and blue cubes; eight in all. Ask the child *'How many red and how many blue cubes have you got?'*

  Ask the child to put two cubes back and then ask what the new total number of cubes is.

- Observe a child playing an addition or subtraction game using objects.

- Give a child three more pencils, when colouring, and ask *'How many pencils have you got altogether?'*

  Any objects used as a resource should be large enough to handle easily.

  If the situation chosen is a group one, ensure that those children who are not being assessed are engrossed in their own work before you start to talk to the child you wish to assess, so that others do not 'jump in' and speak for that child.

What might happen	*What this tells you*
1 Adds and subtracts accurately.	*Achieves the statement.*
2 Doesn't bring the exact number of objects asked for, because he/she forgot.	This does not necessarily mean that the child *cannot* add or subtract. Capitalise on this situation by saying 'I asked for …. You brought me …. How many do you need to take back/How many more do I need?'
3 Re-counts every time a question is asked, rather than mentally adding or subtracting.	*Achieves the statement.* The operation can be practical or mental, and counting from the beginning, rather than counting on, still counts as achievement.

What might happen (cont)	*What this tells you*
4 Adds accurately but subtracts inaccurately.	The context may not have been strong enough to make the intention clear, so try a different context.
	The child may not have developed understanding of subtraction, so provide further experiences. Start with meaningful situations which involve the subtraction of one object (eg 'I've got two pencils – if I ask you to give one to ... how many will be left?'). Let the child carry out the action and check his/her response. Give lots of practice, eg using cubes, straws, etc., building up numbers as the child gains confidence. Again, real contexts, such as eating things, and rhymes such as 'Five little ducks' will help understanding.
5 Adds and subtracts inaccurately.	As above, using similar small numbers for adding.

Developing and extending understanding

- Use real contexts such as those outlined to develop understanding, and encourage making mental predictions and the use of fingers (a very powerful asset!).

- Use number rhymes and songs where adding and subtracting occurs.

- Play games involving addition and subtraction using objects (eg coloured beans, cubes, counters, etc – in various commercially produced maths games books).

- Investigating how many ways to make a number will involve children in addition (eg 'How many different ways can you colour the flag in red and blue?'). See *Bounce To It* for more ideas.

Ma 2/2a Demonstrate that they know and can use number facts, including addition and subtraction.

Related PoS statements
- Knowing and using addition and subtraction facts up to 10.
  (PoS 2/2a)
- Reading, writing and ordering numbers to at least 100 and using the knowledge that the tens digit indicates the number of tens.
  (PoS 2/2b)

About the SoA and related PoS statements

The intended range of number facts, knowledge and use are illustrated in the PoS statements.

PoS 2/2a

The dilemma with this statement is to know what constitutes 'knowing'. Does a child who can add and subtract but who takes time to perform the mental calculations 'know', or should he/she have instant recall of the facts?

The related assessment focuses on the child's ability to recall instantly, although a very short pause is acceptable (even adults need a moment or two to 'sift' the information they have). Instant recall is an important skill, as it allows mental operations to be carried out rapidly when solving more complex mathematical problems.

PoS 2/2b

'Counting' has been omitted from this statement, but is expected as part of the level 1 equivalent.

The ability to count to 100 can be assumed, therefore, if the child achieves the remaining attributes.

PoS 2/2a

Knowing and using addition and subtraction facts up to 10.

Assessment in action

This activity allows you to assess two children at once:

Use Resource Sheet 2 and two numeral (*not* dot) dice between two children (ie each facing a cat). The aim is to cover all the numbers on a cat with counters, by deciding whether to add or subtract the numbers on the dice.

Children take turns rolling both dice, adding *or* subtracting the numbers in order to cover one of the cat spot numbers (eg ⑤ and ① could cover 6 or 4). Children can add for one turn, and subtract for another – they do not have to either add or subtract consistently.

Observe each child having at least three goes while the game is being played, using addition and subtraction.

What might happen	*What this tells you*
1 Clearly knows the various totals when rolling the dice, without needing to count, for both addition and subtraction.	*Achieves the statement* – try level 3a (number facts to 20).
2 Has instant recall for some facts (eg 4+4, 5+5), but needs to count for others (eg 4+5, 4+6).	Needs more experience of number bonds. It may be worth saying 'What is 4+4?, So what is 4+5?' and try to show the child the relationship between the two statements (eg 'It is only one more').
3 Rearranges the dice to subtract.	The child finds it easier to put them in order so that he/she can take the smallest from the biggest.
4 Counts in some way, to total or subtract the numbers.	Needs more practice of number bond games, especially using dice, to encourage quick recall (see extension ideas, below).
5 Has instant recall for addition but not subtraction.	Needs more practice, as above, where subtracting the smallest number from the biggest number is the rule.

Developing and extending understanding

- Games using dice for adding and/or subtracting give children practice of number facts. If the games are played many times, throws which needed to be counted at first soon become learnt. Number bond bingo is an example.

- Play number bond Snap using home-made cards (using + and − only), eg [5–3]. Use cards with bonds to 20 for children who need practice.

- Make cards such as 3+2, 6+1, 10−5, etc. Children play in pairs, seeing if one can work out the answer quicker than his/her partner can find it out on a calculator.

- See Nelson and Cambridge game packs for more ideas.

- Finding patterns in numbers will help recall of bonds (eg 1+9, 2+8, 3+7, etc). See *Bounce To It* for many ideas on repeating patterns.

PoS 2/2b   **Reading, writing and ordering numbers to at least 100 and using the knowledge that the tens digit indicates the number of tens.**

Assessment in action

Part 1   Ask the child to:

1   Cut along the lines of Resource Sheet 3 and order the six numbered cards (cut them out for the child if necessary).

2   Write new numbers on the blank cards, to fit in between the numbered cards. (You may need to ask the child about the missing numbers, to make the task clear – eg 'What are the numbers between 53 and 70? Choose one of them to write on this card.')

3   Order *all* the cards.

Part 2   Point to a card (eg 37) and ask what the *first* number on the card stands for (the child should say '3 tens' or '30'). If this is not understood, give the child some multi-base apparatus (eg Dienes) and ask him/her to use it to show you the number 37. (The point is for the child to produce 3 *tens* and 7 *ones*. Do not use unit-based apparatus, such as Unifix, as the child may simply make a long tower.)

What might happen	*What this tells you*
Part 1	
1 Orders all the cards and writes new numbers correctly.	*Achieves the first three attributes of the statement.* (Reversals of numbers are acceptable.)
2 Orders the six cards, but writes inappropriate numbers on the others.	Has a feel for numerical size, based on the position of the numerals, but needs more experience of place value (eg number-line and calculator activities).
3 Writes new numbers, but cannot order all twelve cards.	Knows how to write numbers to 100, but same as ②.
4 Cannot write appropriate new numbers or order the cards.	The child needs more experiences to develop his/her concept of place value, eg grouping large numbers of objects into tens; making Unifix trails in groups of ten; doing calculator and Dienes games and activities.
	Check also whether the child has developed conservation of number, since he/she will not be able to develop understanding of grouping if he/she cannot conserve.

What might happen (cont)	*What this tells you*

Part 2

1 Says '3 tens' or '30', or shows appropriate multi-base apparatus.	*Achieves the last attribute of the statement.*
2 Says the number itself or the whole number (eg for 37 says 'Three' or 'Three seven') or cannot represent the number in multi-base apparatus.	Needs place value activities as outlined above, especially where objects or Dienes are linked with their number (see extension ideas, below).

Developing and extending understanding

Part 1

- Use the cards to:

  - play Snap! with a partner,
  - make up a game,
  - use ideas from *Count Me In* (games using 0–100 cards).
  - find different ways of sorting the numbers (eg numbers with a 3 in them, even numbers, etc),
  - start off a giant 1–100 square,
  - start off a class 0–100 number line.

Part 2

- Play 'First to 100', using a place value HTU mat, a die, Dienes apparatus and number cards. Roll the die, collecting Dienes units and exchanging for ten rods as the game progresses. At the end of each turn, place the appropriate number cards under the Dienes.

H	T	U
	▯▯▯	▯ ▯ ▯ ▯ ▯
	3	5

- Jump in tens from any number, backwards and forwards on a number line, recording jumps.

- Explore the constant function on a calculator (+10 = = = shows calculator counting in tens).

- See Nuffield Teachers' Books 1 and 2 for some good ideas on place value.

Ma 2

Ma 2/2b   Solve whole-number problems involving addition and subtraction.

Related PoS statements
- Solving whole-number problems involving addition and subtraction, including money. (PoS 2/2c)
- Comparing two numbers to find the difference. (PoS 2/2d)
- Using coins in simple contexts. (PoS 2/2e)

About the SoA and related PoS statements

PoS 2/2c

The use of the word 'problems' suggests that this statement refers to an open-ended use of addition and subtraction, in a problem-solving situation. The related assessment reflects this.

PoS 2/2d

The term 'difference' often confuses children, mainly because they interpret the term literally, basing their interpretations on visual difference. For example, a child who is asked 'What is the difference between 3 and 7?' may think about the symbols themselves and reply 'The three has got curly lines'. If asked the same question while working with sticks or groups of objects, he/she may answer 'Seven is bigger (or longer)'.

PoS 2/2e

This statement implies an understanding of what coins are for and requires the child to demonstrate ability to use them to 'buy' things and to give change.

'Simple contexts' refers, in a classroom context, to the buying and the giving of change, etc, which usually takes place in a class shop. There may, of course, be real situations where children can be observed using coins (eg the school bookshop/tuckshop).

The *use* of the coins, rather than accurate counting, is the focus of this statement.

PoS 2/2c **Solving whole-number problems involving addition and subtraction, including money.**

Assessment in action

This statement lends itself to incidental assessment during normal classroom mathematical activities. The following are examples of the types of activities during which this could be assessed:

- Using a class 'shop', 'cafe' or creative corner where things can be bought and sold:

  (a) 'Buy' three things and ask the child acting as shopkeeper to tell you how much you need to pay. Tell the child to work it out on paper if he/she wants to.
  (b) Give the money and ask for change.

- After a group cooking time, explain that you have worked out that the cost per child is flour 3p, sugar 2p, eggs 4p, etc. Ask the children to find out how much each child needs to pay for their cakes/bread/pancakes. Then ask the child being assessed what change they would need if they brought in, say, 20p.

  Make sure the amounts are manageable (ie up to 20p) and encourage the children to work out on paper, in their own way, if they wish to.

It would be extremely time-consuming to assess all the children at once. Use a situation which is already happening as a learning activity to assess a particular child when you need more information about his/her problem-solving abilities.

What might happen	*What this tells you*
1 Solves the addition and subtraction problem correctly.	*Achieves the statement.* The level of sophistication and economy of method will show you how advanced his/her problem-solving strategies are.
2 Solves the addition, but not the subtraction.	Needs more practical experience of giving change, starting with very small amounts. The shop situation, where you become shopkeeper and count out the change by counting on, would be a good, incidental way of showing the child how change is counted. Encourage children to use their own methods to solve the problem.
3 Sticks to mainly small coins when giving change (eg 10p + nine 1p coins for 19p change).	The child still achieves the statement. *Solving* the problem does not require the most sophisticated method to be used.
4 Finds it difficult to subtract unless he/she uses 1p coins only.	Try limiting the coins to 2p only, so the child has to count in two's in further 'shop' activities.
5 Is unable to solve the addition or subtraction elements of the assessment.	Needs practical experience as above, but in buying first, without adding, and using exact coins.

Developing and extending understanding

- Real-life problem-solving is an excellent vehicle for more open-ended work of this kind. The following starting points will involve children in addition and subtraction as well as finding out, decision-making, estimating, etc:

  - What could we buy with £5 for our class party?
  - How much will it cost to have biscuits and lemonade for the class, so each child has two biscuits and one beaker of lemonade?
  - Look through a catalogue and make a Christmas/present list for your family. How much will you need?
  - How many ways can you make 20p using only 5p, 2p and 1p?
  - How many different ways could you put coins in a slot machine for something costing 5p? 10p?

PoS 2/2d **Comparing two numbers to find the difference.**

Assessment in action

This statement lends itself to incidental assessment, during 'real-life' situations or practical mathematical activities. Some examples of such situations are shown below:

- Ask the class to make two lines when lining up to go into the hall, etc. When the two lines are formed, ask a child *'What is the difference in number between the two lines?'*

- During an activity which involves the child's measuring the lengths of two objects ask *'What is the difference between this length and that length?'*

- While a child is making different length Unifix or Multilink sticks, put two of the sticks side by side and ask *'What is the difference between these two sticks?'*

What might happen	*What this tells you*
1 Correctly tells you the difference.	*Achieves the statement.*
2 Tells you both of the numbers or lengths, rather than their difference.	Ask a further question, eg 'Can you tell me anything else about the difference between them?' if the child is unable to make a correct response, he/she needs more experience of comparing to find the difference using practical situations (see extension ideas below).
3 Gives a literal reply (eg 'That's longer than that one').	Help the child to develop understanding by asking questions such as 'By how many is this stick longer than that stick?' or 'How many ... longer is this one than that one?' Explain that we call the number 'the difference'. Once children can *see* the difference, eg: ⬜⬜⬜⬜⬜⬜⬜ ⬜⬜⬜⬜ 3 is the difference they are more likely to remember this mathematical term.

Developing and extending understanding

- 'Difference' has to be taught, as it is a specific mathematical term, and cannot be 'discovered'. See Nuffield Teachers' Books 1 and 2 for ideas with Unifix. Children need to compare by 'counting on', then being shown that the difference is the amount counted on. This could be in the context of a number line (eg 26 and 22; count on from 22), rows of cubes, centimetre lengths, etc.

  Opportunities to introduce 'difference' could arise from the following:

  – data handling (eg difference between quantities of favourite sweets);
  – body measuring (eg difference between two people's head circumferences);
  – comparing sets (eg difference between the number in each set);
  – comparing groups or lines of children;
  – monitoring plant growth (eg difference between growth of two plants in one week).

PoS 2/2e   **Using coins in simple contexts.**

Assessment in action

This statement lends itself to incidental assessment, while children are engaged in play in a class shop, or are using coins in a real context (eg school bookshop). You will need to become involved in the paying and giving change situation, in order to draw out the assessment.

You should ask the child to pay for something he/she is 'buying' from the 'shop'. The price of the thing being bought is not important but the child should use the correct coins *OR* more, in which case he/she should show that change is expected.

Alternatively, in a play situation, a child may receive money from you and give change. Amounts up to 10p given in payment or as change should be reasonably accurate (ie within 2p).

What might happen	*What this tells you*
1 Uses coins to pay for something (eg gives 5p for something costing 5p, or gives 10p for the same item and asks, or waits, for change) or receives coins as payment, giving change as appropriate (correct within 2p).	*Achieves the statement.*
2 Pays for items with any coins, and does not acknowledge or ask for any change.	The child understands that coins are used as payment, but does not yet equate this with the significance of an amount. However, children may use imitation money sloppily, because they know the context is not real. It would be wise, if you believe this to be the case, to try to observe the child using real money, where change, etc, is likely to be important to him or her.

Developing and extending understanding

- Play situations, especially in created areas such as cafes, shops, etc, encourage children to use money. Act as shopkeeper and buyer with the children, so that they see the conventions of change-giving.

- Exploring combinations of coins helps children to see the relationship between them, eg 'How many ways can you make 10p?'

- Problem-solving can be related to a class party/picnic/outing or similar, where real money is involved, for example 'How much lemonade do we need?' 'How much will it cost?' 'How much will the biscuits cost?'

- Take the children to a supermarket to compare prices, looking for value for money.

- Combinations problems: 'How many different amounts could I spend with 2p, 1p, 5p and 10p if the shopkeeper could give me no change?'

- Use catalogues to choose items totalling £10, make a list for Father Christmas, etc. (use a calculator where appropriate).

Ma 2

Ma 2/2c   Identify halves and quarters.

Related PoS statement
* Understanding the meaning of 'a half' and 'a quarter'. (PoS 2/2f)

About the SoA and related PoS statement

A problem with the PoS statement is the word 'understand'. It would be more appropriate to aim for understanding of the terms, and focus on 'identify' in any assessment.

Common usage of the terms 'half' and 'quarter' are often vague. We frequently refer to half of something when we don't intend this to mean *exactly* half, eg 'I'll be half a minute' or 'Let's have half each of the cake'.

The following activity focuses on the child's ability to understand what a half and a quarter are, and to identify these fractions.

Assessment in action

Discuss Resource Sheet 4 with the child, asking him/her to point out those shapes which show a half, those which show a quarter and any which show some other fraction.

The final section of the sheet is an extension activity.

What might happen	*What this tells you*
1 Identifies all but one of the shapes correctly.	The mistake may be insignificant. Talk to the child about the shape (eg 'show me half of this shape', etc). Decide whether he/she achieves the statement.
2 Identifies only the 'half' shapes correctly.	Talk to the child, as before. If he/she clearly doesn't know what a quarter is, then use this opportunity to give experience of quarters (best with folded paper, string or objects which can be physically divided into quarters, eg a ball of Plasticine or a rod made of Unifix, etc).
3 Identifies all the fractions, but not all correctly.	If the child identifies the 'halves' as halves and the 'quarters' as halves, he/she probably does not have a clear understanding of either. The child probably doesn't understand that halves and quarters and other fractions are different.
4 Identifies all fractions incorrectly and inconsistently.	Make your responses neutral if the child is guessing, rather than making him/her feel 'wrong'. Use this opportunity to develop the child's understanding only if you believe it appropriate.

Developing and extending understanding

- Children should first encounter fractions incidentally, when there is a clear context, for example:

    - folding a piece of paper into halves:
    - dividing the class into groups:
    - having half each of the pencils;
    - sharing the pencils between four, so each one gets a quarter of those in the pot;
    - sharing the Lego, etc.

- Problems such as 'share 4 Plasticine 'sausages' between 5 people' (especially if you can use real ones!) will extend children's understanding of fractions.

- You can help the children's understanding by intervening and using appropriate 'fraction' language (eg 'So you've all got a *quarter* of the pencils we had in the pot'; 'You've shared the biscuits between five of you, so you've each got *one-fifth* of the packet', etc).

- Try the 'half the square' investigation with different sized squares, geoboards, etc.

Ma 2

Ma 2/2d   Recognise the need for standard units of measurement.

Related PoS statements
- Using non-standard measures in length, area, capacity, 'weight', and time; comparing objects and events and recognising the need for standard units. (PoS 2/2g)
- Learning and using the language for common units in length, capacity, 'weight', and time (eg m, 1/2 m, l, 1/2 l, kg, 1/2 kg, day, hour, half-hour). (PoS 2/2h)

About the SoA and related PoS statements

Although the SoA appears to focus on only the last attribute of the first PoS statement, it is probably intended to be interpreted that children will not be able to recognise the need to use standard units unless they *have* engaged in various measurement activities.

PoS 2/2g

The most striking feature of this PoS statement is the large number of attributes. In order to achieve the statement a child would probably need to demonstrate attainment of half or more of these attributes.

Assessment would need to be spread over time, since it would be highly unlikely that any one activity could involve the child in all aspects of measures at once and there would not, therefore, be opportunity to assess all the attributes on one occasion.

The following are examples of the kinds of activities which would allow children to demonstrate use of non-standard measures and of their ability to recognise the need to use standard units. They tend to be paired or group situations which require an observation or dialogue with the child being assessed in order to assess attainment. It is always advisable to confirm assessments with ongoing observations of children working with measures.

PoS 2/2h

This statement relates to the previous one, except that area is excluded.

The assessment activity combines the two statements, as the language used would be likely to occur in the context of using measures.

Assessment in action

Length

Ask two or three children, of varying size, to find out *how many footsteps it is from one place to another* or *how many handspans wide their table is* (make sure the number is within their counting range). When they have finished, discuss their findings with them. Ask them what would need to be used to make sure the distance was always the same, no matter who measured it. (If there is not enough size variation, you may need to be involved.) Ask general questions about how length is measured, to determine whether they know the appropriate language.

Area

Ask two children to each find out the area of an identical shape or a tile, by covering it with buttons (of varying size) and counting them.

Talk to the children afterwards, asking how many buttons they each used. Ask the child being assessed how we could make sure that the answer/area would always be the same, or what we would need to use to ensure this.

Capacity

Ask two children to try to find out how many small cupfuls of water, sand or dried peas will fill a larger container. They should both use identical large containers but lots of different sized small containers.

Talk to the children afterwards, asking how many 'cupfuls' the capacity was/the container held. Ask the child being assessed how we could make sure, or what would need to be used, so that the answer would always be the same. Ask general questions about how liquid is usually measured, to determine whether they know the appropriate language.

Weight

Ask two children to find out how much something weighs, using shells, conkers, books or any other non-standard unit. They should both weigh the same object and use identical units (eg both use shells).

Talk to the children afterwards, asking how many units the objects weighed. Ask the child being assessed how we could make sure, or what would need to be used, so that the answer/weight would always be the same. Ask general questions about how mass is usually measured, to determine whether they know the appropriate language.

Time

Ask two children to find out how long it takes for another child to write his/her name ten times. They should devise a method to use to time the writer, but should each carry it out separately.

Talk to the children afterwards, asking how they timed it and also asking them to share their results with you. Ask the child being assessed how we could make sure, or what would need to be used, so that the answer would always be the same. Ask the children general questions about how time is measured, to determine whether they know the appropriate language.

What might happen	*What this tells you*
Length	
1 Tells you two different numbers, eg 'I made it 13 footsteps and Anna made it 15', *and* says you would have to use only one person's footsteps or something like a ruler.	*Achieves PoS 2/2g – length only.* Check Ma 2/3e, which is the next stage in the strand.
2 Tells you two different numbers, as above, but says that you could take just one person's number or that you could take a number in between the two they found.	Can use non-standard measures, but does not perceive the problem in terms of standardising the measure. It is seen as a numerical problem rather than a matter of the measure being used. The child needs experience of a variety of problems such as this, especially where a larger group of children are all tackling the problem and where the purpose of asking them to solve the problem leads them to need accurate results.

What might happen (cont)	*What this tells you*
3 Works out the distance to be the same number for both children (eg adjusted the size of the steps they took so that they both made it the same).	Does not have a clear understanding of the importance of accuracy in measuring, and is possibly responding literally to the question 'How many' by providing one answer. Purposeful contexts, where accuracy is essential, will help develop this understanding.
4 Talks about any *two* of miles, kilometres, feet, inches, centimetres, metres, yards, in a way which shows an understanding of use (eg uses miles when talking about long distances).	*Achieves PoS 2/2h – length only.* Check Ma 2/3e, which is the next stage in the strand.
5 Only mentions one or none of the above, showing understanding.	Assess again in more informal contexts (eg via stories, informal discussion, other measurement contexts) in case the child needs a more meaningful context. If the child still does not achieve, he/she needs more discussion and real-life situations for the terms to be taken on.

Area

1 Performs the task, and is able to tell you that you would have to use buttons of the same size.	*Achieves PoS 2/2g – area only.* Check Ma 2/3e, which is the next stage in the strand.
2 Tells you two different numbers, but says you could take a number between them.	As Length ☐2 above.
3 Worked out the area to be the same between them by spacing the buttons accordingly.	As Length ☐3 above.

Capacity

1 Tells you two different numbers *and* says that you would have to use cups which were exactly the same size, or just one cup.	*Achieves PoS 2/2g – capacity only.* Check Ma 2/3e, which is the next stage in the strand.
2 Worked out the capacity to be the same between them by using less or more sand/ water/dried peas or some other method.	As Length ☐3 above.
3 Talks about any *two* of pints, litres, 1/2 pint, millilitres, gallons, in a way which shows an understanding of their use (eg uses gallons when talking about petrol or buckets of water).	*Achieves PoS 2/2h – capacity only.* Check Ma 2/3e.
4 Only mentions one or none of the above, showing understanding.	As Length ☐5 above.

What might happen (cont)	*What this tells you*
Weight	
1 Tells you two different numbers and says that the units would all have to be the same size.	*Achieves PoS 2/2g – weight only.* Check Ma 2/3e, which is the next stage in the strand.
2 Tells you two different numbers, and says you would need to swap some of the small ones for big ones until the number was the same.	As Length ⟨2⟩ above.
3 Works out the weight to be the same between them by adjusting the size of the units used.	As Length ⟨3⟩ above.
4 Talks about any *two* of stones, pounds, ounces, tons, kilograms, grams, in a way which shows an understanding of their use (eg uses ounces when talking about very small amounts).	*Achieves PoS 2/2h – weight only.* Check Ma 2/3e.
5 Only mentions one or none of the above, showing understanding.	As Length ⟨5⟩ above.
Time	
1 Tells you two different ways of timing and says that you would both have to use the same method, or use standard measures (eg seconds/minutes).	*Achieves PoS 2/2g – time only.* Check Ma 2/3e.
2 Does not appear to see a problem with using different methods.	Needs more experience of timing exercises, and discussion. Real-life situations will make learning easier (eg different children find out how long it takes to do something).

Developing and extending understanding

- Purposeful activities which involve children finding their own ways of measuring lead naturally to a need for standard units. For example:

  - How far does a vehicle travel down a ramp?
  - Which class walks the furthest distance to the hall each morning?
  - How much material do we need to buy to make curtains for the play corner?
  - How much material do we need to cover the table?
  - How much does this box hold?
  - How much does your flask hold?
  - How much weight can the paper bag hold before it tears?
  - Who can write the fastest?
  - How long does it take us to run round the playground?

  These tasks will also extend understanding, as there is a problem to be solved and the level of accuracy required can be discussed with you.

Ma 2

Ma 2/3a   Read, write and order numbers up to 1000.

Related PoS statements
- Reading, writing and ordering numbers to at least 1000, and using the knowledge that the position of a digit indicates its value. (PoS 2/3a)
- Learning and using addition and subtraction facts to 20 (including zero). (PoS 2/3b)

About the SoA and related PoS statements

The PoS statements augment the SoA in terms of specifying ordering to 1000 and a full understanding of place value.

PoS 2/3a

The emphasis of the second part of the statement is on *use*. In the assessment activity, the six given numbers have been chosen so that ordering can only be achieved if such knowledge is used. If the child can order these numbers, the last attribute is automatically achieved.

PoS 2/3b

This statement refers to the learning, by rote, of number bonds such as $11 + 7$, $9 + 8$ and all others which total 20 or less. The use of these bonds would be evident in any numerical operation by the children.

The related assessment focuses on the child's ability to recall instantly, although a very short pause is acceptable (even adults need a moment or two to 'sift' the information they have). Instant recall is an important skill, as it allows mental operations to be carried out rapidly when solving more complex mathematical problems.

Interestingly, the use of zero is mentioned here but not at Level 2. Zero is a number often left out by teachers, but is important for children to include. Zero is a place-holder and 'completes' the pattern of our number system (eg 0, 10, 20, 30 ...).

PoS 2/3a

Reading, writing and ordering numbers to at least 1000, and using the knowledge that the position of a digit indicates its value.

Assessment in action

Ask the child to cut along the lines of Resource Sheet 5, **order** the six numbered cards and **write** on the blank ones *any* number which would come between each of the six cards, then **order** all the cards. (You should cut out the cards for any child having difficulty with this.)

What might happen	*What this tells you*
1 Writes appropriate numbers and orders all twelve cards.	*Achieves the statement.*
2 Orders most of the cards but confuses 719 with 791.	The teen numbers are very confusing, because we say '*nine*teen', sounding the 'nine' first. The child expects the nine to be written first, as all other numbers have that pattern. Pointing this out often helps. (See extension ideas for level 2.)
3 Has some numbers in the wrong order, but self-corrects when asked to read the numbers out.	Either a careless slip, or the understanding of place value is not matched to the child's mental and spoken abilities. Needs more experience of writing numbers.
4 Writes a new number wrongly (eg 30076 for 376) although reads it as 376 and puts it in the correct order.	Understands the value of spoken numbers, but needs more experience of place-value games which link with writing numbers (see level 2a Dienes game), and of the use of a calculator in solving problems.
5 Writes new numbers but cannot order the twelve cards.	Knows what three-digit numbers look like, and would probably be able to order the numbers if it could be done by looking at the first digit only. Needs more games and use of a 0–1000 number line, calculator and multi-base apparatus when solving problems. *Achieves the first two attributes.*
6 Cannot write new three-digit numbers or order the cards.	Try level 2a. If the child achieves this, he/she needs experience as described above.

Developing and extending understanding

- Set up a 0-1000 number line (Harcourt Brace Jovanovich supply 0–100 lines which can be stuck end to end and written on).

- Give children starting-point numbers to jump in 10s or 100s forwards and backwards, for example:

  37   137   237, etc

  recording their jumps as they go. Spotting the patterns helps children see how our number system is a repeating sequence; once the pattern is seen, children can normally jump in 100s orally ('37, 137, 337, etc).
  Having this mental ability enables children to perform addition and subtraction sums by jumping along a number line, and eventually doing this mentally. Understanding the pattern also helps children see how the numbers are written.

- see also the *Count Me In* games (HBJ), which can be extended to 0–1000.

PoS 2/3b   **Learning and using addition and subtraction facts to 20 (including zero).**

Assessment in action ▬▬▬▬▬▬▬▬▬▬▬▬▬▬▬▬▬▬▬▬▬▬

This activity allows you to assess two children at once:

Part 1   Use Resource Sheet 6a between two children, each facing a Bingo board. (Alternatively, cut through the centre line so that the children have a card each.) The aim is to cover three numbers in a line, or to cover every number on the baseboard, as you prefer.

Each child takes turns rolling the special dice (see resources list), *adding* the numbers shown, and covering that number on his/her baseboard with a counter.

Observe each child having at least three goes while the game is being played, to assess their instant recall of addition bonds to 20.

Part 2   This is exactly the same as the addition-bond bingo except that Resource Sheet 6b baseboards and the second set of special dice (see resources list) are used. This game is played by *subtracting* the smaller number from the bigger number rolled each time.

Resources

- Resource Sheets 6a and 6b for each pair of children being assessed.

- Two *addition dice* (make by numbering wooden cubes with a felt pen/cover cube in masking tape and label sides):

  0, 1, 2, 3, 4, 5 and
  10, 11, 12, 13, 14, 15

- Two *subtraction dice*:

  0, 1, 2, 3, 4, 5 and
  14, 15, 16, 17, 18, 19

- A pile of counters or Unifix cubes.

  Organise the games as part of maths activities. They can be used to practise number bonds as well as for assessment.

What might happen	*What this tells you*
1 Is observed using instant recall in making numbers, using addition and subtraction bonds to 20.	*Achieves the statement.*
2 Has instant recall for some facts (eg 10+5, 15–0, etc) but needs to count on for more difficult bonds.	Needs more experience of bonds and patterns. It may be worth saying 'What is 10+5? So what is 11+5?' and try to show the child the relationship between the two statements (eg 'It is only one more').
3 Has instant recall for addition bonds but not subtraction.	Addition bonds are easier to remember and seem to arise more often than subtraction bonds. More experience is needed, especially in seeing patterns (see extension ideas, below).
4 Counts in some way, to add or subtract the numbers.	Needs more practice of number bond games, especially using dice, to encourage quick recall.

Developing and extending understanding

- Games using dice for bonds need to be played many times. Throws which are intially counted soon become 'learnt'.

- Make cards such as $\boxed{15 + 3}$ $\boxed{12 - 4}$, etc. Children play in pairs, seeing if one can work out the answer quicker than his/her partner can find it out on a calculator.

- Finding patterns in numbers will help children find strategies (eg 11+1, 11+2, 11+3, etc).
  See *Bounce To It* for many ideas on number patterns.

- Use Resource Sheets 6a and 6b to:

  - find how many ways each number can be made using the dice (look for systematic ordering);
  - use for *multiplication* bingo. Which numbers would need to be written on the dice?
  - make up new baseboards and new dice using any of the operations (+, −, ×, ÷);
  - explore the probability of getting a particular number most often.

Ma 2

Ma 2/3b Demonstrate that they know and can use multiplication tables.

Related PoS statement
- Learning and using multiplication facts up to 5×5 and all those in the 2, 5 and 10 multiplication tables. (PoS 2/3c)

About the SoA and related PoS statement

The difficulty in assessing this SoA is that a child may demonstrate knowledge of some of the table facts while solving a problem, but not enough to enable you to be sure he/she knows them all. 'Know' in this SoA is assumed to mean instant recall, and refers to the table facts described in the PoS statement.

The following assessment aims to assess knowledge of the range of multiplication facts stated in the PoS statement in the context of a mapping exercise, and to assess their use in a number investigation.

Assessment in action

Part 1

Give the child Resource Sheet 7 and explain the task. Observe the child mapping the first five numbers, to see whether he/she 'knows' the table facts.

Part 2

As an activity during normal classroom maths: ask the child to find out how many different numbers can be made between 1 and 50 using only these numbers: 2, 3, 4, 5, 10 and a $\times$ sign. Say he/she should record these in his/her own way.

Use the child's work to assess 'use' of table facts, or alternatively visit the child while he/she is working and talk about his/her work.

If the child has difficulty, and clearly does not know the table facts, give him/her a calculator. The task will no longer be suitable for assessment of this SoA, but will be a good learning activity.

What might happen	*What this tells you*
Part 1	
1 Maps most of the facts correctly and without first working them out in some way.	*Achieves the first part of the statement.*
2 Maps only a few facts correctly, with or without working out.	Needs more practice of table facts in number investigations, calculator and dice games, and their use to promote understanding.
3 Maps the facts correctly, but works them out first.	It is important to 'know' table facts, but being able to work out the product in some way indicates a good understanding of what table facts are. Needs more experience of activities such as those suggested above.

What might happen (cont)	*What this tells you*
Part 2	
1 Is observed using knowledge of table facts to record the different numbers. (Finding *all* the numbers which can be made is not important for this assessment.)	*Achieves the second part of the statement.*
2 Works out the products without 'instant recall' while investigating.	Needs practice as above. However, the child should be encouraged and praised for finding his/her own ways of working out the products and investigating the problem.

Developing and extending understanding

- Explore the constant function on the calculator, for example:

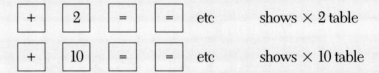

| + | 2 | = | = | etc | shows × 2 table |
| + | 10 | = | = | etc | shows × 10 table |

- Investigate different products with limited numbers, as in Part 2, but using a calculator.

- Play Multiplication Bingo, multiplying two dice together to cover the numbers.

- Look for patterns in table facts in a 100 square.

- See the comments on developing 'instant recall' in the assessment activities for PoS 2/2a and PoS 2/3b above.

Ma 2/3c   Solve problems involving multiplication or division.

Related PoS statements
- Solving problems involving multiplication or division of whole numbers or money, using a calculator where necessary. (Pos 2/3d)
- Understanding remainders in the context of calculation and knowing whether to round up or down. (PoS 2/3e)

About the SoA and related PoS statements

PoS 2/3d

The reference, in the PoS statement, to the use of a calculator implies that the ability accurately to multiply or divide using standard methods is not required. In order to use a calculator to solve a problem which involves multiplication or division, a child would need to know what multiplication and division is, how it is used and when it is used. He/she would also need to be able to estimate the answer, in order to check that the right keys had been pressed. The precise skills of multiplying and dividing are outlined elsewhere: this statement focuses on the use of the *processes* of multiplication and division, in order to solve a more complex problem.

Pos 2/3e

This statement is not intended to be assessed in a practical context, as 'remainders' cannot be rounded up or down if they are real objects, hence the inclusion in the statement of the phrase 'in the context of calculation'.

PoS 2/3d

Solving problems involving multiplication or division of whole numbers or money, using a calculator where necessary.

Assessment in action

The following problems will involve children in multiplication and possibly division:

- Using only three 2p coins, find out how many 2p coins will completely cover your desk.

- Find out how many chairs will fit in the (rectangular) hall.

- Find out how many cubes will fit in this tray – you only have five to find out with.

- Find out how much it will cost for the class to have lemonade and biscuits tomorrow.

- In planning for stock next year I want every child to have a full set of coloured pencils. There are 12 pencils in a box costing 80p a box and most colours are available. Work out what I need to order and how much it will cost me.

Children should use whatever resources they want and should be encouraged to solve the problem *in their own way*. Ask each child being assessed to put down on paper in some way *how* they worked it out. Make your assessment by observing the child, by asking for a description of how the task was tackled, or by looking at the child's recording.

What might happen	*What this tells you*
1 Solves the problem in his/her own way, using multiplication and division. (You may need to assess on two separate occasions.) The use of repeated addition is not enough.	*Achieves the statement.*
2 Solves the problem, but uses a long-hand method, such as repeated addition (eg counts all the rows as a long addition sum: $6 + 6 + 6 + 6 + 6$ instead of 6×5).	Children need to solve problems using their own methods, as that is what allows them to make sense of the problem. Real understanding develops through such methods, at which point the quicker 'standard' way can be introduced by the teacher. Standard methods introduced too early are often not understood and cannot be applied to problems, hence the often-heard question 'Is it an add or a subtract?', etc.
3 Gets 'involved' with the materials provided and loses sight of the problem.	Encourage the child's own developments, but remind him/her of the initial problem.

What might happen (cont)	*What this tells you*
4 Finds it difficult to solve the problem.	Intervene appropriately, asking questions which break the problem down, such as: 'What could you do first?', 'How many cubes will fit in this space?', 'How many biscuits should each child have?' 'How can you find out how many biscuits in a packet?' Encourage and praise all suggestions, and suggest that the child 'tries it out', finding a different way if it doesn't work out at first.

Developing and extending understanding

Recent research has shown that even very young children, given highly contextualised situations, can use large numbers effectively and use problem-solving strategies to a high level of sophistication. The key to this seems to be in allowing children to invent their own methods, share their different strategies, use mental methods and calculators freely and later be introduced to standard conventions.

The books *Children and Number* and *Maths with Reason* deal with these issues in detail. *Piers is lost* and *Mathematics with seven and eight year olds* show examples of children working at 'pure' maths and real-life maths problem-solving. *I hate mathematics* is one of the many collections of worthwhile starting-points for mathematical exploration. See the reference notes on page vii for further examples.

PoS 2/3e   **Understanding remainders in the context of calculation and knowing whether to round up or down.**

Assessment in action

Give the child/children the following calculator investigation:

- Enter a number between 50 and 100 in the calculator.
- Divide it by 3.
- Round you answer up or down.
- Divide the new number by 3.
- Round your answer up or down to the nearest whole number.
- Divide the new number by 3, etc.

What number do you get to? Try this starting with different numbers. Do you always end at the same number?

Observe the child rounding up or down, or look at the child's recording to assess this SoA.

What might happen	*What this tells you*
1 Correctly rounds off most of the numbers.	*Achieves the statement.* You will have much more information about the child's problem-solving abilities.
2 Incorrectly rounds off or just copies the the same number.	Make sure the child understood the task. If not he or she needs a combination of activities involving calculator activities which focus on remainders (see the extension ideas) and explanations about how to round off.

Developing and extending understanding

- Calculator investigations help to develop understanding of decimal remainders, for example: Which two numbers multiplied together, make 10?

  Encourage the children to try any two numbers to start with, recording the numbers they get, then to adjust the numbers they go on to try according to their results.

Ma 2/3d   Make estimates based on familiar units of measurement, checking results.

Related PoS statements
- Making estimates based on familiar units. (PoS 2/3f)
- Recognising that the first digit is the most important in indicating the size of a number and approximating to the nearest 10 or 100. (PoS 2/3g)

About the SoA and related PoS statements

The two PoS statements have been linked as they both relate to the making of an estimate. However, the first statement ('*making estimates based on familiar units*') is best assessed in the context of a measuring activity. The context will then determine the degree of accuracy required of the estimate, and will therefore be a more valid and reliable assessment. This statement, therefore, is assessed with other PoS statements in the activity following this one.

PoS 2/3f

The 'familiar units' should correspond with the estimate (eg petrol in gallons, the length of a carpet in feet, yards or metres). The SoA has the additional requirement of 'checking results'. This amounts to the child testing out the prediction, using appropriate resources.
This statement is assessed with PoS 2/3j, k.

PoS 2/3g

The difficulty concerning the first attribute of this statement is in recognising whether or not a child actually looks at the first digit when ordering numbers. If a child is able to order three-digit numbers, it can be assumed that this has been done.
'Approximating' should be interpreted here to mean the ability to round up or down to the nearest 10 or 100.

PoS 2/3g

Recognising that the first digit is the most important in indicating the size of a number and approximating to the nearest 10 or 100.

Assessment in action

Give Resource Sheet 8 to the child you wish to assess and explain the task clearly. Children should know already that we round up from 5.

What might happen	*What this tells you*
1 Completes the Resource Sheet, with not more than two errors overall in the rounding off sections.	*Achieves the statement.* (The ordering can be from lowest to highest or vice versa.)
2 Completes the Resource Sheet, with more than two mistakes.	Talk to the child about the sheet making sure the errors are not just careless 'slips'. If the child has not attained the statement, try some ordering games and activities and tasks involving rounding up and down within the context of a problem. For example: 'Roughly how many do you think it will be: 20, 30, 40?'

Developing and extending understanding

- Children will need experience of rounding up and down in real-life contexts, so that there is 'human sense' in making an approximation. Some appropriate contexts might be shopping, talking about temperature, using recipes and talking about quantities.

- See also the *Count Me In* games (HBJ) for lots of ordering games and other ideas.

Ma 2

Ma 2/3e   Interpret a range of numbers in the context of measurement or money.

Related PoS statements
- Using decimal notation in recording money. (Pos 2/3h)
- Recognising negative whole numbers in familiar contexts, eg a temperature scale, a number line, a calculator display. (Pos 2/3i)
- Using a wider range of metric units of length, capacity, 'weight', and standard units of time. (PoS 2/3j)
- Choosing and using appropriate units and instruments: interpreting numbers on a range of measuring instruments, with appropriate accuracy. (PoS 2/3k)

About the SoA and related PoS statements

PoS 2/3h

The statement intends that a child should *know* the correct method of recording, even if he/she does not use it exclusively (eg 50p is more commonly used by children than £0.50).

PoS 2/3i

This statement refers to children *recognising* negative numbers. This could be conveyed by the child saying that the number is 'below or less than zero' or calling it 'minus x', or simply saying that the number 'comes before zero or 1'.

PoS 2/3j

The word 'wider' in this statement refers to the use of both large and small units within the same measure (eg kilometre, metre, centimetre, millimetre). The statement is vague as to *how many* units and measures would need to be used in order for a child to achieve it.

PoS 2/3k

The word 'choose' implies that children must have access to a wide variety of measuring devices from which to make a selection. The kinds of measuring instruments available should include tape measures, rulers, metre sticks, surveyor's tapes, bathroom scales, balances, spring balances, kitchen (pressure) scales, a variety of metric and imperial containers, stop-watches and clocks.

'Interpreting numbers' simply means that the chld can read off a measurement from any scale. 'Appropriate accuracy' means to the nearest displayed unit.

PoS 2/3h   **Using decimal notation in recording money.**

Assessment in action

There are a number of occasions when children talk or write about or use imitation or real money in the classroom. Choose one of these to ask the child to write the amount/price in the correct way. You could give an example, to clarify the task for the child. The following are examples of occasions when recording could be appropriate:

- Labelling goods in a class shop;

- Planning a meal or party menu;

- Finding out how much things cost (eg comparing prices of biscuits in different shops);

- Doing a class pocket-money survey;

- Writing a letter (with prices) to Father Christmas.

What might happen	*What this tells you*
1 Writes some amounts using decimal notation:	As this is evidence that the child *knows* the convention, he/she *achieves the statement.*
2 Writes mainly in his/her own way (eg 1 pound 20p, £1.20p, etc).	Once the child is confident in using his/her own method of recording, simply show the convention, describing it as the correct way which is used in shops, etc.
3 Writes amounts incoherently (eg £10050p/705p).	Ask what the amount says. The child will usually say an amount which makes sense (eg for this example 'One hundred pounds and fifty pence/seventy-five pence'. This is the equivalent to the stages in children's writing. The child needs more place-value experience also linking to real money before conventional recording is explained.

Developing and extending understanding

- Handling money and writing amounts in real contexts will develop a child's understanding of money more effectively than money problems or exercises on paper.

- Capitalise on school bookshops, dinner money collection, charity collections, etc, as contexts for children becoming involved in the counting.

- Link jumping in 10s on the 0-100 number line with counting up 10p's (eg 10, 20 30, 40p, etc).

- Playact as shopkeeper in order to show how change is conventionally given, starting with very small amounts and using coins of just two or three different values.

PoS 2/3i

Recognising negative whole numbers in familiar contexts, eg a temperature scale, a number line, a calculator display.

Assessment in action

Show how the constant function on the calculator (eg [+] [1] [=] [=] [=], etc) enables the calculator to 'count' in ones every time [=] is pressed (check first that it can perform this function – some calculators do not).

Ask the child to press [2] [0] [–] [1] [=] [=], etc, and to carry on, then tell you what happened to the numbers.

What might happen	*What this tells you*
1 Says something which indicates an understanding of the place of the numbers, eg 'They go below zero', 'They go less than zero' '–1 is after zero. That's how numbers go. It does it both ways'.	*Achieves the statement.* The comment will show the level of the child's understanding (eg the last comment showed that the child has a feel for the concept of infinity).
2 Says 'The numbers go backwards' or 'There's a line in front of the numbers'. Says 'Goes down then it goes up'.	Has noticed a change of some kind, but is not clear what is happening to the numbers. Needs to do more work using number lines which extend to negative numbers, and to do more calculator exploring, recording the numbers either horizontally or vertically, for example: $$\begin{array}{c} 3 \\ 2 \\ 1 \\ \hline 0 \\ -1 \\ -2 \\ -3 \end{array}$$ Games where a counter goes backwards and forwards or up and down from a central point help develop the concept.

Developing and extending understanding

- Children develop understanding of negative numbers mainly through using a caclulator and number lines which extend to below zero. Research shows that children used to using calculators have little or no difficulty in extending the number line below zero.

  When negative numbers arise, zero becomes an important place-holder.

- Use the constant function to explore numbers on the calculator (eg + 10 =, + 100 =, etc).

- Find out how a thermometer works and test the temperature of various places in the school/classroom.

- Play a prediction game – make up a sum and your partner predicts whether the outcome will be above or below zero. Check on a calculator.

PoS 2/3j	**Using a wider range of metric units of length, capacity, 'weight', and standard units of time.**
PoS 2/3k	**Choosing and using appropriate units and instruments; interpreting numbers on a range of measuring instruments, with appropriate accuracy.**
PoS 2/3f	**Making estimates based on familiar units.**

These three statements have been linked for this assessment, as they can be easily and efficiently assessed in one activity. However, the assessment will be more valid if it is reinforced by ongoing observations of the child's measuring over a period of time.

As in the other assessment activities, the following assessment can be used as a check when you are not sure of a child's ability.

Assessment in action

Set up a table with four objects on it: one for 'guess the weight', (eg a box of something), one for guess the length (eg a piece of ribbon or string), one for 'guess the capacity' or 'guess how much it holds' (eg an empty jug) and a sandtimer for 'guess how long it takes'. Make sure a wide variety of measuring instruments are accessible, including a stopwatch.

Ask the child being assessed to write down, or tell you, what their guess for each object is (assesses PoS 2/3f).

Then ask him/her to use whichever measuring instrument/s he/she chooses to find out the exact answer for each object, and to write them down.

When this is done, ask the child to choose a *different* measuring instrument to *check* the answer, and write it down again. (In the case of the stopwatch, the child should simply check it again.)

You should try to observe the moment when the child reads off the measurement. If this is not possible, ask the child to show you later.

You will also need to ask the child to read off the exact time from an analogue and a digital clock for complete achievement of PoS 2/3k.

What might happen	*What this tells you*
1 Makes an appropriate estimate for each object (eg using grammes, kg, ounces or pounds for the weight).	*Achieves the first part of Ma 2/3d (PoS 2/3f).*
2 Makes an inappropriate estimate for one or more objects (eg uses centimetre for the weight).	*Is not ready for this assessment. Check with the assessment for level 2. Make sure that the child did not simply make a careless slip.*
3 Measures the objects twice, each time with a different instrument (except for time), reading off the measure accurately each time, either orally or in writing.	*Achieves Ma 2/3d, as the measuring counts as testing the prediction. Also achieves PoS 2/3j and 2/3k.*

What might happen (cont)	*What this tells you*
4 Can only measure accurately using one measuring device.	Has probably not had enough experience of using the range of measuring instruments. Children need to be shown how to read most scales.
5 Measures inaccurately each time (eg says 10cm when it is 9.2cm or 9cm 2mm).	Is not ready or has not been taught enough for this level. The child needs to be shown how millimetres relate to centimetres, etc, and how to read off accurately.

Developing and extending understanding

- Using the varied measuring instruments, children should be encouraged to solve problems involving measurement. Children will want to experiment with different measuring devices from an early age, if they are not made to feel that they must be able to use them 'properly' (just as children browse through books before they can read them). Once a child has recognised the need to use standard units, he/she should be motivated and ready to use and be shown the standard units on different measuring instruments.

Ma 3

Ma 3/1a Devise repeating patterns.

Related PoS statement
- Copying, continuing and devising repeating patterns represented by objects/apparatus or single-digit numbers. (PoS 3/1a)

About the SoA and related PoS statement

Experience of making and recognising repeating patterns provides an important foundation for children. Our number system consists of a series of repeating patterns, and many mathematical formulae originate from the identification of a 'pattern'. The following assessment focuses on repeating patterns using either objects or one-digit numbers.

Assessment in action

1 Choose one of the following activities:

Unifix, Multilink, Clixi, beads or other coloured apparatus
Begin a two-coloured line using the chosen materials (eg red, yellow, red, yellow) and ask a child to carry on making the same pattern. Say you want this to be used to ask someone else to 'Guess the Pattern'.
If the child does this successfully, ask him/her to use those materials to make up a repeating pattern line of his/her own, to be used for the guessing game.

2 *Numbers*
Begin by writing the pattern 2, 1, 2, 1, and then ask the child to carry on writing the same pattern.
If he or she does this successfully, ask the child to make up his/her own repeating number pattern and to write it for you to see. (Make sure the child is able to write numerals if you choose to assess the statement in this way.) Put this in the context of a guessing game, as above.

What might happen	*What this tells you*
1 Continues the pattern line correctly and makes up his/her own repeating pattern.	*Achieves the SoA.* Check level 2a, which is the next SoA in this strand.
2 Chooses a repeating number pattern using numbers with confusing shapes (eg 3535) so that the child becomes muddled.	Ask for another pattern using two different numbers, or alternatively ask the child to *tell you* how the original pattern would continue (about ten 3,5's would probably mean he/she understood!).
3 Continues the pattern for a while, but then uses different colours or numbers.	Check that the child understood the task. Children sometimes get bored and want to use new colours or numbers to inject new stimulation. If this might be happening, ask the child to tell you how the colours would continue if the line went on for a long way. If the child is not sure, give him/her lots of opportunities to make some (see extension ideas, below).

What might happen (cont)	*What it tells you*
4 Continues the pattern correctly but cannot make up his/her own line using a repeating pattern.	Needs encouragement to choose, initially, two colours or two numbers, to make pattern. He or she also needs lots of practical activities involving making repeating patterns (see the extension ideas).

Developing and extending understanding

- Making body patterns, with the children in a circle so that they can see one another (eg first child stand up; next child sit down; next child stand up; next child sit down ...), is excellent experience for developing understanding.

    Extend these kinds of experiences by exploring whether the pattern will go on 'for ever' round the circle with x number of children. Try changing the pattern (eg stand up; stand up; sit down; stand up; stand up; sit down; etc).

- Make repeating patterns with 2-D and 3-D shapes. *Using* some of the children's 2-D patterns to make attractive borders for other work helps provide consolidating experience.

- Encourage the children to make up their own repeating patterns and then to see if a friend can continue them.

- Children can be asked to make up their own repeating patterns and then explain the 'repeat' to you or to another child (eg if they make 23122312231223 ... can they explain that the repeated part is 2312?)

- See *Mathematics Their Way,* by Mary Baratta-Lorton, for many ideas and background reading on the importance of pattern. She discusses the importance of repeating patterns as the beginning of an understanding of the repeating patterns in our number system.

- See the BEAM pack *Odds and Evens* for repeating pattern ideas.

Ma 3/2a   Explore number patterns.

Related PoS statements
- Exploring and using patterns in addition and subtraction facts to 10. (PoS 3/2a)
- Distinguishing odd and even numbers. (PoS 3/2b)

About the SoA and related PoS statements

The second PoS statement is linked with exploring number patterns because the process of identifying odd and even numbers involves children in finding patterns (eg 1, 3, 5, 7/2, 4, 6, 8).

PoS 3/2a

The use of the words 'explore' and 'use' in this statement implies that the patterns in number facts should be explored in the context of a number investigation. An awareness of patterns in number facts would be evident if the child connected different combinations as being part of a limited set (eg 'I've got 9 + 1, 6 + 4, and 5 + 5 but I've still got to find the other ways to make 10).

PoS 3/2b

The ability to distinguish between odd and even numbers depends on recognising whether the last digit is either odd or even. The related assessment activity focuses on sorting odd and even numbers.

PoS 3/2a

Exploring and using patterns in addition and subtraction facts to 10.

Assessment in action

First ask the child to find how many ways he/she can make the number 8, using any numbers from 0 to 10 and + and – (let the child use paper and pencil, counters or other objects in two colours, or whichever method he/she finds easiest).

Ask the child to show you his/her 'results' when finished. You may need to ask 'Have you found all the ways?' and 'Can you see a pattern in the numbers?' (This would be relevant if the child had written, for instance, 9–1 is 8, 10–2 is 8, 11–3 is 8.)

The aim of the assessment is for you to observe the child 'seeing' the patterns in the combinations, either by explaining all the ways you could make 8, or by listing the combinations in an ordered way.

What might happen	*What this tells you*
1 Finds ways to make 8 and explains or sees the pattern. The following are examples of achievement in trialling: 5 and 3 → 8 'I added the cubes and I tried 3 and 5 → 8 to make 8.' 4 and 4 → 8 'Did you find all the ways?' 6 and 2 → 8 'Yes.' Because I counted with 7 and 1 → 8 the cubes.' 0 and 8 → 8	*Achieves the statement.*
9 – 1 = 8 '9 take away 1 is 8, 10 take away 2 10 – 2 = 8 must be 8, 11 take away 3 is 8...' 11 – 3 = 8 'Can you see a pattern?' 12 – 4 = 8 'Yes. It goes 1 2 3 4 5 6 7 8 9 and 13 – 5 = 8 9 10 11 12 13 14 15 16 17.' 14 – 6 = 8 'Did you find all the ways?' 15 – 7 = 8 'No. You could keep going and take 16 – 8 = 8 away more numbers.' 17 – 9 = 8 'When would you stop?' 'Never.'	
2 Does not seem aware of patterns, even though can make some combinations.	Talk to the child, perhaps asking 'What numbers haven't you used yet?' Using eight cubes and a simple divided board helps to contain the problem. Ask the child to 'throw' the cubes onto the board and count how many land in each segment, keeping a record of each throw.

Developing and extending understanding

- Explore number bonds (see ideas from AT2 assessments). 'Combinations' problems offer lots of possibilities, for example:
  'How many different ways can the flag be coloured using red and blue?'

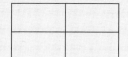

  'How many different ways can the red, yellow and blue cars park in the car park?'

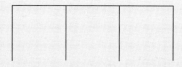

- Try money combinations, using imitation coins, eg *'How many ways can I spend 5p?'*

- See also *Workjobs* and *Bounce To It* for lots of combinations and baseboard ideas.

  Encourage children to be systematic in their work, so the patterns become more evident.

PoS 3/2b   **Distinguishing odd and even numbers.**

Assessment in action

Give the child Resource Sheet 9. Ask him/her to cut through the lines and then sort the cards into odd and even numbers. The child should be encouraged to do this in his/her own way.

What might happen	*What this tells you*
1 Sorts the number cards into odd and even sets or groups.	*Achieves the statement.*
2 Sorts the number cards into odd and even sets, but with some cards included in in the wrong sets.	Ask the child to check that all the numbers are in the right sets. If the child makes no alterations then he/she has some concept of odd and even (probably knowing which of the numbers below ten are odd and which are even) but has not yet realised the 'pattern' in the last digits by which oddness or evenness can be determined (see the extension ideas, below).
3 Uses 2 × table (counting in twos) as a check after sorting.	*Achieves the statement.* The child may know the difference between odd and even numbers, but simply needs to be sure.
4 Uses inappropriate logic (eg '24 is even because 2 and 4 are even', '30 is odd because 3 is odd').	The child needs experience of equal and unequal towers and sets. The significance of the last digit is obviously not clear yet.
5 Needs to use counters to decide whether the numbers are odd or even.	This shows that he/she knows how to work out an odd or even number, but does not know instantly, so is not aware of the significance of the last digit. Number line jumping in 2s from 0, then 1, will help consolidate this (see below).
6 Is not able to sort the numbers.	The terms 'odd' and 'even' need to be taught. This should follow experiences involving odd and evenness in a practical context.

Developing and extending understanding

- See BEAM pack *Odds and Evens.*

- Using Unifix or Multilink 'towers', ask:

  'Which 'towers' break in half evenly? Keep a record of what you discover.'

  'Which numbers will 'break' into pairs and which will not? Record the numbers.'

- Explore house numbers.

- Look for repeating patterns when moving along a number line, for example:

  'Start at 0. Jump, in twos, along the line.'
  'Start at 1. Jump, in twos, along the line.'

- Colour in every second number on a 100 square and look for patterns.

- Make a growing pattern on squared paper, recording the total number of squares each time, for example:

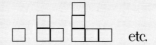 etc.

Ma 3

Ma 3/2b   Recognise the use of a symbol to stand for an unknown number.

Related PoS statement
- Understanding the use of a symbol to stand for an unknown number. (PoS 3/2c)

About the SoA and related PoS statement

The essence of this SoA is 'use of a symbol'. The context does *not* have to be in the context of a mathematical operation, using addition, subtraction, multiplication or division. A simple sequence of numbers is sufficient and the following assessment reflects this.

Assessment in action

Give the child Resource Sheet 10 and explain the task.

What might happen	*What this tells you*
1 Completes the Resource Sheet correctly, giving at least one combination of numbers which total 6.	*Achieves the SoA.*
2 Completes line 1 correctly, but not the other lines.	Make sure the child understood the task. You may need to talk it through with some children. If he/she did understand the task, then needs more experience of using symbols in various contexts.

Developing and extending understanding

- Symbols used in the media (road signs, weather, symbols, picture symbols in shops) could be explored to help the children understand the purpose of symbols.

- Codes are excellent for stimulating interest in symbols. For example, make a game of encouraging the children to write one another messages, using pictures to represent missing words or using symbols to represent letters of the alphabet.

- Make up games using symbols instead of a number.

Ma 3/3a Use pattern in number when doing mental calculations.

Related PoS statements
- Developing a variety of strategies to perform mental calculations using number patterns and equivalent forms of two-digit numbers. (PoS 3/3a)
- Explaining number patterns and predicting subsequent numbers. (PoS 3/3b)
- Recognising whole numbers divisible by 2, 5 or 10. (PoS 3/3c)

About the SoA and related PoS statements

The SoA simply provides a broad statement which the PoS statements clarify in more detail.

PoS 3/3a

The main point of this statement is that children should be able to calculate *in their own way*. Children who have only been 'allowed' to perform standard sums will not have the confidence or the experience and control over numbers to be able to manipulate them. Using a variety of resources, children should first be encouraged to find totals and differences between numbers using their own invented methods. These should be valued as correct. Standard notation should be introduced once children have control over the calculation in this way.

Since the calculation is performed mentally, it can be difficult to determine whether the child did 'use number patterns, etc' to reach his/her answer, since the child may be unable to express in words the precise mental method he/she used. This can sometimes make assessment of the two parts of this statement difficult, even if a child's answer is correct.

PoS 3/3b

The term 'explain' implies that a child should be able to explain *how* the numbers in a pattern are developed (eg 'they go up in fives').

PoS 3/3c

The word 'recognise' means that the child should be able to identify that, for instance, 25 is divisible by 5. Division does not usually occur as frequently as multiplication in problem-solving, so the related assessment reflects this.

PoS 3/3a

Developing a variety of strategies to perform mental calculations using number patterns and equivalent forms of two-digit numbers.

Assessment in action

This statement lends itself to incidental assessment, when a child is engaged in a problem which involves mental calculation.

Ask the child *how* he/she worked out a calculation involving two-digit numbers.

The child may need encouragement to reveal a method which is not standard. You should make it clear that *any* way of working something out is good, if the child feels comfortable with it.

If an opportunity to assess does not arise naturally from other work the child is doing, give the child a 'sum' to work out mentally (eg 29 + 33) and explain you would like to find out how he/she works it out. This is best done with several children, at sharing time perhaps, so that they can explain and compare their different methods. Sharing in this way would give a child who was not confident, the opportunity to listen and to begin to build on his/her understanding without feeling that he/she *had* to participate.

Ask the child to describe another way to work out the total, to assess the 'variety of strategies.'

What might happen	*What this tells you*
1 Explains how the operation was mentally calculated, demonstrating strategies other than a 'visual sum'.	*Achieves the statement.*
2 Explains the calculation in terms of a 'mental sum' (eg 'I added the 9 and 3 and carried the ten ...')	A child who has mentally calculated in this way, even though the answer he/she arrives at may be correct, is not demonstrating achievement of this statement. (In fact it is unusual to find a child performing a mental calculation in this way. Children, and adults, usually use quite diverse methods when performing mental calculations.) Give the child other opportunities to talk about methods used for calculation, as one context does not necessarily give a reliable assessment.
3 The child cannot explain how he/she worked it out	Needs more opportunities for activities in which talking about maths is an integral part. Begin by encouraging the child to talk about how he/she carries out various practical tasks. Provide opportunities for children to share talk of this kind. When introducing problems involving mental calculation, ensure that the numbers are very small to begin with.
4 Does not offer another way of working it out, but clearly understands other children's methods.	The joint discussion may have exhausted the methods, so this will count as achievement. The child need not actually do the calculation to show knowledge of a variety of strategies, but simply explain a method (eg you could jump up from the 23, etc).

Developing and extending understanding

- Encourage children to compare different methods of recording and to solve problems using mental calculation.

- See *Mathematics with Seven and Eight Year Olds,* by Marion Bird (Mathematical Association/West Sussex Institute). This shows a variety of children's different methods in solving the same problem.

PoS 3/3b   **Explaining number patterns and predicting subsequent numbers.**

Assessment in action

Give the child Resource Sheet 11 and explain the task.

Ask the child how the numbers developed, eg for the first two lines on the Resource Sheet: *'How are the numbers getting bigger in this first line?'* or *'How did you know which numbers came next in the second line?'*

What might happen	*What this tells you*
1 Completes the number patterns correctly and can explain how the numbers develop, eg 'They go up in twos'.	*Achieves the SoA.*
2 Completes the number patterns incorrectly.	Needs number-line games and sequencing experiences. Check that the child can make repeating patterns (level 1), as this is the natural starting-point for number patterns. The child may also not be sure of the numbers from 0 to 100, so understanding of this should be checked.

Developing and extending understanding

- Look at growing patterns in a variety of contexts and at the number patterns which emerge from them:

  - encourage the child to build 'triangular' numbers from Clixi or on squared paper, for example:

     etc

  - encourage the children to build successively larger squares using apparatus or squared paper, for example:

    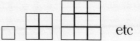 etc

- See *Bounce To It* for lots of of ideas for number-pattern experience.

PoS 3/3c   **Recognising whole numbers divisible by 2, 5 or 10.**

Assessment in action

Give the child Resource Sheet 12 and explain the task.

What might happen	*What this tells you*
1 Correctly joins the numbers to the appropriate circles (one error is acceptable).	*Achieves the statement.*
2 Maps some numbers which link to more than one circle (eg 20 is divisible by 2, 5 and 10) to only one circle.	Make sure the child understands the tasks, as he/she may think the numbers must only link to one circle.
3 Maps most of the numbers incorrectly.	Needs further experience using multiplication and division in problem-solving situations. Check Ma 2 (level 3b) for knowledge of multiplication facts for 2, 5 and 10 multiplication tables.

Developing and extending understanding

- See the extension ideas for Ma 2/3b, page 46.

Ma 3

Ma 3/3b   Use inverse operations in a simple context.

Related PoS statement
- Dealing with inputs to and outputs from simple function machines.
  (PoS 3/3d)

About the SoA and related PoS statement

'Inverse operations' refers to inputs and outputs, positive and negative, forwards and backwards, etc, so in algebraic terms the two statements refer to the same process.

A 'simple function machine' is a device for changing something into something else. This could be for shapes (eg turns them upside down) or other aspects of maths.

Assessment in action

Give the child Resource Sheet 13 and explain the task. Any two of the four machines can be completed, as they are all different contexts, any of which may be 'preferred' by the child. Choose whether you ask the child to attempt them all, or fewer.

Calculators and counting aids (eg cubes) can be provided.

What might happen	*What this tells you*
1 Correctly processes the inputs and arrives at the appropriate outputs for *two* of the machines.	*Achieves the statement.* Children may need to use counters or calculators to achieve the output. The important thing is that they understand the function machine.
2 Correctly processes only two of the three inputs required for a machine.	Ask the child to check his/her work. If still incorrect, the child needs more practice and application of the operation in question. The 'machine' is simply a device for processing a number, so using the machine should not be a problem if the child has a good understanding of operations with numbers (eg addition, subtraction, multiplication and division) in practical situations.
3 Cannot process the inputs.	Make sure the child understands the task (ie what the machine *does*). Give the child some very simple function machines using small numbers and simple operations (eg 1 [+2] →)

Developing and extending understanding

- Children could make up their own function machines for others to do.

- Make up function machines with an input and an output and guess what the function was. This involves more problem-solving strategies.

- Try a function involving more than one operation.

- Function machines like the parking meter involve more complex computation, so more able children could tackle various kinds (eg other costs, speeds, times, etc).

Ma 4

Ma 4/1a Talk about models that they have made.

Related PoS statements
- Sorting and classifying 2-D and 3-D shapes using words such as 'straight', 'flat', 'curved', 'round', 'pointed', etc. (PoS 4/1a)
- Building 3-D solid shapes and drawing 2-D shapes and describing them. (PoS 4/1b)
- Using common words, such as 'on', 'inside', 'above', 'under', 'behind', 'next to', to describe a position. (PoS 4/1c)

About the SoA and related PoS statements

The SoA assumes that children will have experience of the first two PoS statements so that they can talk about shapes. It may be necessary to have different contexts for children to need to use the prepositions in Pos 4/1c, such as building a Lego model, bridges or making boxes.

PoS 4/1a

Sorting here means according to any criterion which is related to shape (eg shapes which are round/not round; shapes which are triangles, squares and circles, etc). The next developmental link in this AT is at level 3, where children are asked to sort in different ways. 'Classifying' means the sets must be labelled or named, in written or oral form.

PoS 4/1b

The building of 3-D solid shapes is important because, through the experience, children have the opportunity to learn about which shapes will stack, which surfaces can take the weight of another shape, etc. The word 'describe', with reference to 3-D shapes, could be an oral or a written response, and is likely to be oral at this stage. The description itself does not have to be very sophisticated. The following would be at the level expected: 'It's got straight sides', 'It's got pointy edges', 'It looks like an ice cream cornet'.

PoS 4/1c

This kind of positional language happens naturally in children's talk if the context demands it. (Bilingual children may have an understanding of such words in their home language, but may not be able to express the words in English. This can be assessed via the child's home language, if you have access to a bilingual support adult.)

PoS 4/1a

Sorting and classifying 2-D and 3-D shapes using words such as 'straight', 'flat', 'curved', 'round', 'pointed', etc.

Assessment in action

This statement lends itself to incidental assessment, when children are already engaged in activities or games involving sorting shapes. Observe a child sorting, and ask him/her to explain *how* the shapes have been sorted. The shapes can either be sorted separately (ie 2-D shapes then 3-D shapes) or mixed up together.

(Collaborative work, although usually encouraged, makes it difficult to determine who thought of the sorting criterion, if you need to assess.)

What might happen	*What this tells you*
1 Sorts the shapes in a consistent way (eg all the flat shapes and all the not-flat shapes, with all the shapes in the appropriate sets).	*Achieves the statement.* Decide whether the child could re-sort the shapes (level 3a). He/she may do this without prompting, so check the notes for the level 3 assessment. Any method of sorting is appropriate for this level.
2 Sorts the shapes by colour.	Colour often dominates with sorting. Try giving the child a variety of shapes in one colour only. This should focus attention on properties of shape.
3 Cannot sort the shapes consistently and tends to play or make pictures.	See extension ideas, below. Children with particular learning difficulties might be over-stimulated by the objects. If you think this is the case, limit the sorting to one small collection only (eg buttons).

Developing and extending understanding

- See Mary Barratta-Lorton's *Mathematics Their Way* for much in-depth support in relation to children learning to sort, for example:

    - use buttons, lids, keys, etc., which are all the same but with small differences, so that children are not confused by attributes;
    - use the buttons, for instance, and ask: *'Which one is your favourite?'*, *'Why do you like it?'*
    - Whatever the child says (eg 'shining') ask *'Are there any more like that? Where shall we put them so these are the shiny buttons and these are the...?'* (children usually say 'not shiny' for dull).

- Talk to children about the sets they have made. Ask questions like: *'Where shall we put the buttons that are shiny **and** green?'* (if, for example, the child has made two sets: red buttons and shiny buttons). Children in this situation usually first put the shiny green buttons between the two sets, for example:

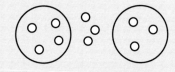

Ask how the objects can go into both sets at once. Children often physically move the two sets closer and place the intersection objects along the boundaries, for example:

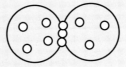

At this stage an intersection can be shown to children.

- Do not give children a limited number of set rings, as this will determine for them how many sets they must sort into. It is better to have lots available, as well as string or wool which can be used to partition sets.

- Play sorting games (eg Feely bag sorting) and the Yes/No game:

  In pairs:

  - one of you decide on a criterion, eg 'rough';
  - take objects out of a box placing them on the *yes* sheet if they are rough or the *no* sheet if they are not;
  - continue silently until your partner has guessed what your criterion must be.

- Recognise, use and encourage sorting in topic work (eg insects which fly/ have hairy legs/have long antennae).

PoS 4/1b   Building 3-D solid shapes and drawing 2-D shapes and describing them.

Assessment in action

Part I   'Building 3-D solid shapes' lends itself to incidental assessment, when children are exploring or playing with 3-D shapes.

Observe the child building with the shapes. Ask him/her to build a tall tower if this is not being done.

Part 2   The second attribute 'Drawing 2-D shapes and describing them', needs to be set up.

Ask the child to draw a shape picture (this could be related to the class topic) for someone else to 'find' the shapes in. Suggest he/she could draw circles, squares, oblongs.

When the picture has been drawn, ask the child to talk to you about it. Ask questions about the shapes which will encourage the child to talk about them, such as '*How is the circle different to the square?*' (pointing), '*Tell me about this shape*' (pointing to an oblong), '*What shapes have you used?*'

What might happen	*What this tells you*
Part 1	
1 Builds with the 3-D shapes, possibly making complex constructions.	*Achieves the first attribute* and probably understands much about the properties of 3-D shapes (eg support and balance, etc).
2 Builds with the 3-D shapes, replacing certain shapes when nothing will balance on top of them.	*Achieves the first attribute.* The statement does not expect expert building. The child is learning about the properties of shapes by experimenting with building.
3 Does not build with the shapes.	The child may have manipulative difficulties. Use big, easy-to-handle shapes. You may need to start the tower off to encourage the child, in case the child is not motivated, or suggest the building of something else.
Part 2	
1 Draws some shapes and describes them simply to you (eg 'It's got four sides', 'It's like a long square' ('It's round').	*Achieves the second attribute.* The description should be general and does not have to include *all* the properties of the shape. The extent of the child's description will give you information as to how much about the shape he/she knows. The drawings need to be recognisable shapes, but not necessarily accurate. The child's drawing may indicate knowledge of symmetry – see Ma 4/3b.

What might happen (cont)	*What this tells you*
2 Draws shapes but with not enough variety (eg all rectangles), and describes them in some way.	The child may need your intervention to prompt the drawing of new shapes (eg 'Can you draw a different shape?', 'Could you draw a triangle now?'). If this is successful, the child will achieve the attribute. If not, the child needs more experience of handling and talking about different shapes. The naming of the shapes is not necessary at this level.
3 Draws a shape picture, but does not describe the shapes well enough (eg, 'What is the difference between a triangle and a circle?', 'They look the same', 'That one hasn't got any corners and that one has').	You may need to ask more specific questions to focus the child's attention (eg 'Tell me what a triangle looks like'). The child may 'know' how the shapes are different but not have the vocabulary to describe them. This may be especially true of bilingual children. Feely bag activities would be especially useful, starting with natural objects such as stones, shells, etc, which are more easily described.
4 Draws patterns or pictures rather than 2-D shapes (eg, doodles, scribble pictures). He/she may describe the patterns appropriately.	The focus of this attribute is 2-D shapes, so 'patterns' are not enough. The child should be praised for the drawings, and possibly asked if he/she can now draw some maths shapes. Look carefully at the drawing, because there may be shapes in it that you could ask the child to describe (eg, 'I can see a square - can you find another one?'). The child may also have manipulative problems, but the statement does not allow for this. Drawing around large 2-D shapes may help small motor control.

Developing and extending understanding

- Shape games (eg, feely bag descriptions) are excellent for developing language.

- See the BEAM pack *Hollows and Solids* for many investigative open-ended starting points.

- Polydron or Clixi enable children to create exciting 3-D shapes, and learn about faces.

- Straws and Plasticine are useful for making nets of solid shapes.

- Use junk boxes to make 3-D models to link with your class topic.

- In pairs, take a shape each and take turns saying how the shapes are the same. After this, do the same for how the shapes are different. Try taping these descriptions for analysis later.

- Wrapping parcels in different ways helps children explore shape properties.

- Sorting shapes also helps children focus on specific properties.

PoS 4/1c   **Using common words; such as 'on', 'inside', 'above', 'under', 'behind', 'next to', to describe a position.**

Assessment in action

This statement lends itself to incidental or activity-based assessment. The following are examples of situations where you should be able to assess it:

● Listen to children talking together when setting out or tidying up the creative corner.

● Listen to children talking together when putting play objects/people into a toy house or vehicle. The children will need to use positional language in these situations and you will hear them ask questions such as 'Where shall we put the table?', 'Who shall we put next to the driver?'

● Say *'Make a pattern with these 4 bricks so that your friend can't see it. Now tell your friend where to put her bricks so that her pattern looks the same as yours'* (You will need to set up a small divider between the children to stop child 1 pointing and saying 'put it there', etc.)

Make sure your presence does not inhibit the children if you choose to assess by observation.

What might happen	*What this tells you*
1 Uses appropriate positional language, as described in the PoS statement or similar.	*Achieves the statement.* Has a developing understanding of these prepositions and of how to use them.
2 Uses some positional words, but uses inappropriate words at times (eg 'behind' instead of 'below', 'into' instead of 'inside').	Knows some words but has not yet heard and linked them with a context or with other positional words. (The child's home language should be used if the child does not have the vocabulary in English.)
3 Points to the correct place but cannot 'find' the right word.	Needs more opportunities to develop this vocabulary
4 Uses words like 'put it there' when you feel sure the child has a vocabulary of positional language.	Children don't always use the vocabulary that they have, and the teacher knows they have, if the context does not specifically require it. You may need to set up a more structured 'game', as in the example, to make a reliable assessment.

Developing and extending understanding

- Strong contexts and a sense of purpose will stimulate the use of positional language. The assessment examples and the following are some contexts which should encourage appropriate talking.

  - playing, with another child, with sand or water;
  - exploring, with others, constructional apparatus, both large and small;
  - making a model with a friend;
  - making a picture/collage, together with a friend;
  - practical science tasks (eg using a ramp to see how far a vehicle can travel) undertaken in a small group.

    In all these you might need to join in and to interact with the children to introduce new positional words. Do this by asking where something should go, then speaking the correct words back to the child, but not as a correction which might inhibit confidence. For example, if the child says 'I'm going to put it there', you could say 'So it's going to go *beside* the elephant'.

    Bilingual children will find games a useful way of developing mathematical vocabulary, especially if certain 'key' words are repeated. Stories with repeating refrains are also excellent for helping develop vocabulary. *Goldilocks and the Three Bears* and *Jack and the Beanstalk* are examples of stories with lots of positional language. (See Nuffield Bronto books for maths 'stories'.)

- Using Logo or Roamer will encourage the development of positional language.

- Children can make up 'treasure hunts' for each other, leaving messages saying where to look next, eg 'behind the bin'; 'in the desk', etc.

- Play a game in twos – one is given a simple symbol to describe to the other child, who is not able to see the symbol and who has to draw it according to the first child's directions.

  Something like:

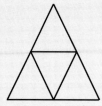   or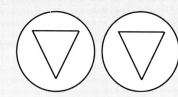

  would encourage positional words such as 'inside', 'next to', 'beneath', 'under', 'below' etc.

- Legodacta is another excellent resource for encouraging positional language.

Ma 4/1b Follow or give instructions related to movement and position.

Related PoS statement
● Giving and understanding instructions for movement along a route.
(PoS 4/1d)

About the SoA and related PoS statement

This SoA refers mainly to physical, whole-body movements, but could also refer to the context of moving a robot or drawing a shape from given instructions. The understanding of directional language, such as 'straight', 'curved', 'go forwards', 'backwards', etc, is the underlying focus of the statement.

Assessment in action

This SoA lends itself to incidental assessment during a PE or a dance lesson.
   Ask the children to move in various ways, eg in a straight line, along a curved line, in a zig-zag line, etc.
   Observe the child/children being assessed.
   Ask the children to get into pairs and to take turns giving instructions to their partners (as above) if you wish to extend the assessment.
   Although this activity can be done with the whole class, you will have to limit the number of children you can assess by deciding how many you can actually observe at one time.

What might happen	*What this tells you*
1 The child moves appropriately in response to one of the instructions.	*Achieves the statement.* The way the child moves for the other instructions will indicate how much he/she knows about direction and lines, or where the vocabulary is not understood.
2 The child does not appear to differentiate between different kinds of movement, for you to be able to assess his/her ability to move along a line, but can give instructions to a partner.	Many children have poor physical control or some other special need such as limited hearing or vision. The child may be able to *draw* straight or curved lines more easily, so drawing can be used to make this assessment. The vocabulary may not be familiar to the child, in which case you will need to find opportunities for the child to experience the word 'in action'.
3 Can follow the instructions, but cannot give them.	The child may lack confidence or have forgotten the appropriate words. With more experience of being the 'receiver' of instructions, he/she will probably remember. A child who is shy might be more confident in a more intimate setting (eg giving instructions to a friend who is pretending to be a 'robot' during a play situation).

Developing and extending understanding

- Use skipping ropes placed in various shapes on the floor for children to walk along.

- Introduce the notion of straight and curved lines when talking about 2-D and 3-D shapes.

- Children can play, in pairs, at being robots.

- Use geoboards with elastic bands to explore different kinds of lines.

- Curved stitching combines straight and curved lines.

- Make border patterns using alternating line shapes.

Ma 4

Ma 4/1c Compare and order objects without measuring.

Related PoS statement
- Comparing objects and ordering objects and events without measuring, using appropriate language. (PoS 4/1e)

About the SoA and related PoS statement

The use of 'appropriate language' emphasises the importance of children developing mathematical language and explaining their thinking, and implies the use of words such as '*long, longer, longest*'; '*heavy, heavier, heaviest*', etc.

The inclusion of 'events' means that the concept of time passing is also assessed. Comparative language would be words such as 'sooner', 'later', 'before', 'after', etc.

Another important word to note is 'objects'. Since pictures of objects can be distorted or drawn to different scales, children will find that making any comparison of the dimensions of the objects in pictures will be more difficult, since they can be misleading. It is also important that comparisons should be made between real objects which are juxtaposed, as distance can distort perception of size.

It is easier to compare than to order objects, especially when there are more than three objects, as a child needs certain organisational skills to carry out the ordering.

Assessment in action

This SoA lends itself to incidental assessment, during practical mathematical activities. The following are examples of the kinds of situations in which children might demonstrate achievement of this statement. As with many statements of attainment, assessment will be more reliable if made on several occasions and in different contexts.

- Putting some containers in order of size, height or capacity (perhaps whilst playing with sand).
- Finding out who is the tallest in the class.
- Ordering/organising the books on the shelf or in the book corner.
- Deciding the weight of six parcels.
- Finding out who has the longest hair.
- Finding out which cards will fit in which envelopes.
- Building the tallest tower possible with twelve different shapes.
- Collecting information about children's birthdays.

What might happen	*What this tells you*
1 Compares one object to another, in order to see which is smaller/taller, etc, and can order at least three objects.	*Achieves the statement.* Listening to children talking about the ordering will inform you about the extent of their vocabulary.
2 Can compare and order two objects only.	Ordering more than two objects requires spatial and organisational skills. The child needs practice with three objects in a variety of situations, in a collaborative, supportive context.
3 Cannot differentiate size, etc, between two objects.	This may indicate a child who has special educational needs. A strategy for developing awareness is to focus on extremes (eg a very large and a very small box/ball, etc, to be put in order). Gradually make the difference less obvious and introduce an 'in-between' object.

Developing and extending understanding

- Encourage the children to listen to and discuss stories which use comparative language, eg *Goldilocks and the Three Bears, Jack and the Beanstalk*, etc). Bilingual children benefit especially from repetitive use of language, as in *Goldilocks*.

- Use comparative words in questions to the child when he/she is involved in a suitable activity, so that he/she begins to learn how they are used (eg 'Who is taller – you or me?'; 'So, who is tallest?'; 'Which holds the most?').

- Always use the correct language when talking 'back' to the children. For example, if a child says 'That one is more big than that one', then, before moving on to make another comment, help the child to see the correct use of comparative language by saying something like 'So that one is bigger'.

- Encourage comparisons between objects in sorting activities.

- Take two objects or 3-D shapes and list/discuss their similarities and differences (tape two children doing this to obtain detailed information about their use of comparative language).

Ma 4

Ma 4/2a   Use mathematical terms to describe common 2-D shapes and 3-D objects.

Related PoS statements
- Recognising squares, rectangles, circles, triangles, hexagons, pentagons, cubes, rectangular boxes (cuboids), cylinders and spheres and describing their properties. (PoS 4/2a)
- Recognising right-angled corners in 2-D and 3-D shapes. (PoS 4/2b)

About the SoA and related PoS statements

Although the first PoS statement refers to 'recognising' shapes only, the SoA asks for the use of 'mathematical' terms, so the naming of the shapes is required for assessment.

PoS 4/2a

The shapes listed in the first PoS statement can be either regular or irregular, since the statement doesn't say *only* regular. This is important, since children need to know that (for instance) *any* five-sided shape is a pentagon, not only those five-sided shapes which have sides of equal length.

Children are usually familiar with the listed shapes, but remembering their names can be a problem.

'Their properties' are mathematical characteristics, such as 'four straight sides, four right angles, twelve edges, etc'.

PoS 4/2b

This statement implies that a child should be able to recognise what a right-angled corner looks like, rather than know about right angles and degrees, etc. A 'right angle' can be taught without expecting knowledge of degrees, by using a quarter turn on a clock face or a set square.

PoS 4/2a

Recognising squares, rectangles, circles, triangles, hexagons, pentagons, cubes, rectangular boxes (cuboids), cylinders and spheres and describing their properties.

Assessment in action

The assessment is in two parts: the first uses Resource Sheet 14, which asks the child to identify 2-D shapes and describe them; the second involves a 'feely bag' game which is used as a vehicle to encourage children to identify and describe 3-D shapes.

Part 1

Give the child Resource Sheet 14 and explain the task.

When this is completed, point to two of the shapes (one at a time) and ask *'What can you tell me about this shape?'* , *'What does it look like?'*, *'Can you describe it to me?'*

Part 2

Fill a material bag (a drawstring bag is ideal) with some cubes, some cylinders and some spheres. Make it clear to the children that the objects in the bag are mathematical shapes from the 3-D shape box.

Ask the children to take turns 'feeling' in the bag for a shape and describing it to the group. The first child in the group to guess what the shape is has the next turn with the feely bag.

What might happen   ## *What this tells you*

Part 1

1 Puts a cross on each shape (one error is acceptable), and describes two of the shapes (eg 'It 's like a box', 'It's got four sides', 'It's got four corners').	*Achieves the first part of the statement.* The child's use of language in describing the shapes should tell you how much the child perceives about their properties. Statements such as 'It's like a box' will need to be qualified by the child.
2 Puts a cross on each shape but cannot describe them 'mathematically'. For example, says 'It's the pattern on the curtain' or 'It's a hat' or 'It's a shape'.	The child is focusing on the context of the picture, so you will need to ask further questions in order to give him/her the best opportunity to show you what he/she knows, eg 'Look at the *shape* of his hat – what can you tell me about the shape?'
3 Puts crosses on different 'shapes', such as the rabbit's tail or the magician's shoe.	Make sure the child understand the task. Read the shape names out, as he/she may be having difficulty with the reading, rather than with the mathematics. If the child still cannot identify the shapes, he/she does not 'know' what they are called. Shape names are mathematical facts, and ultimately need to be remembered (just like mathematical symbols and numerals).

What might happen (cont)	*What this tells you*

Part 2

1 Describes two of the shapes (eg 'It's all round', 'It's like a coke-can/dice', 'It's got all flat sides') *and* names two of the shapes.

Achieves the second part of the statement. The child's use of language in describing the shapes should tell you how much the child perceives about their properties.

2 Describes the shapes inadequately, eg 'It's big', 'It's hard'.

Ask the child to tell you more about it (eg 'How many sides does it have?'; 'Does it have any corners?'). The child may not have developed the appropriate vocabulary yet, and will need more involvement in games like this, where the language of shapes can be developed.

Developing and extending understanding

- See the BEAM packs *Hollows and Solids* and *Triangles and Quadrangles*.

- Words like 'hexagon' and 'pentagon' are difficult to remember. Help the child to make links by introducing other words such as, for example, pentomino and pentathlon, and encourage *them* to seek out such words and to try to discover their meanings.

- Play shape games – for example, where the dice is labelled with shape names and the child has to place the appropriate shape on a matching baseboard. Such games help the children to link the name of the shape with its appearance.

- Talking about shapes is very important, as in the 'feely bag' game, as this promotes thorough examination of the properties. Try asking two children each to choose a 3-D shape and then to compare them. Encourage them to find as many things as they can which are the same and which are different about their two shapes.

- Tower building involves finding out about the properties of shapes, so this makes a good exploration activity.

- Making and wrapping boxes, etc, helps children develop understanding about the properties of those shapes, including their surfaces and nets.

- Use Clixi, Polydron, Multilink, etc, to create 3-D shapes. Problems such as 'How many different ways can you join six cubes together?' will help develop understanding and extend the children's thinking.

PoS 4/2b   **Recognising right-angled corners in 2-D and 3-D shapes.**

Assessment in action

This statement lends itself to incidental assessment, while children are engaged in sorting 2-D and 3-D shapes.

Ask the child after he/she has explained how the shapes have been sorted, if he/she can show you/point to some corners which are right angles or square corners.

You may need to ask the child to do this in a quiet place where other children will not intervene.

What might happen	What this tells you
1 Indicates one right-angled corner on a 2-D shape and one on a 3-D shape.	*Achieves the statement.* You could ask more to see how much the child knows (eg 'What is a right angle?', 'What is an angle?').
2 Does not know what a right-angled corner is, or points to any corners.	'Right-angled corners' are another mathematical fact which children need to know – so show the child a right-angled corner and explain that we call these kinds of corner 'right-angled corners'. Experience of using and talking about right angles will then help the child remember the name.

Developing and extending understanding

- 'Roamer' and 'Pip' are excellent for making turns using a computer. Logo uses degrees, but the word 'right angle' could be introduced when children are using it, thus providing a meaningful context.

- Develop understanding by asking the children to make quarter turns with their whole bodies while, for example, moving like robots, during PE.

- Ask children to look at different shapes and try to explain the difference between the corners.

Ma 4

Ma 4/2b   Recognise different types of movement.

Related PoS statements
- Recognising types of movement: straight (translation), turning (rotation). (PoS 4/2c)
- Understanding angles as a measurement of turn. (PoS 4/2d)
- Understand turning through right angles. (PoS 4/2e)

About the SoA and related PoS statements

The SoA in this case is a broad statement which encompasses the ideas expressed in the PoS statements.

PoS 4/2c

This statement is rather complex, and needs simplifying. The statement states that children should be able to recognise the different *types* of movement, not necessarily know the names (in brackets) which are there to define the types of movement for the teacher. A straight movement consists of moving something in a straight line from one place to another in any direction. A turning movement is a rotation of something, on its axis, of up to 360°.

PoS 4/2d

The notion of angle means knowing that an angle consists of a turn. Knowledge of degrees is not required at this stage, but simply the word 'angle' to indicate a turn. This assessment should only be used if children are familiar with whole, half and quarter turns.

PoS 4/2e

This statement implies that the turning could be of a physical nature. The following assessment reflects this. It seems a particularly difficult Statement for this level, however, as there are many skills needed to turn through right angles apart from an understanding of angle itself, so children may not succeed as you would hope. It is expected that children being assessed for this statement will have used and are familiar with right angles.

PoS 4/2f

Understanding the conservation of length, capacity and 'weight'
This statement has no apparent link with the related SoA. When the original ATs were streamlined, the 'measures' SoAs were divided between the new ATs. This statement was placed here because the working party felt that there was no clear place to put it, but in practice it would seem advisable to assess PoS 4/2f in the context of measuring/number rather than shape and movement.

Assessment activities for the statement are provided on page 94.

PoS 4/2c

Recognising types of movement: straight (translation), turning (rotation).

Assessment in action

This statement contains two elements, so they have been incorporated into a game in order to allow you to assess them at once.

Land the Rocket game
Rules (*Aim*: to get your rocket to land on a planet)
You will need:

- A labelled die (use masking tape or sticky labels on a large wooden cube):

  - 'Turn' (on 3 faces)
  - 'Straight 2 squares' (on 3 faces)

- Resource Sheet 15 as a baseboard.

- A cut-out rocket for each player, coloured in both sides (a different colour for each child).

1 Players place the baseboard in front of them, and each player places his/her rocket on any one of the outlined inside squares.

2 Players take turns rolling the die, reading the instructions (or you may need to read them out) and moving their rocket appropriately. 'Turn' must be a half or whole turn. Rockets cannot move diagonally.

3 The first player to get 'home' is the winner.

You will need to observe the children making the moves to make the assessment. Do not *teach* the different movements immediately before the game. The point of the assessment is to find out if the child *knows* how the movements are made.

Once a child has been assessed you should teach the moves in order to allow the child to play the game and not feel unsuccessful, but an assessment too soon after teaching is of little worth, as the child may forget the moves after a short time, in which case the child does not 'know' them.

What might happen	*What this tells you*
1 Is observed making the correct movements in the game.	*Achieves the SoA.*
2 Makes some correct movements, but cannot make them all (eg does not know how to 'rotate half a turn'), or does not do so consistently.	The child needs practical experience of the unknown movement (eg turning activities as described for the assessments and extensions of PoS 4/2d and PoS 4/2e, if rotation is the problem).
3 Is unable to make any of the moves correctly.	Teach the child in order to help him/her play the game, but do not try to assess as a result of this. Be sensitive to the child's ability to make the moves at all, as this is a difficult game.

Developing and extending understanding

- Make new rules for moving on the board (eg change board, change die, etc).

- Make up a game which involves diagonal moves.

- Investigate 'ominoes', eg 'How many ways can you join five squares together?' (pentominoes – five squares; omino – one square; dominoes – two squares; etc) – children usually colour in lots of different shapes. Cut them out and rotate to see how many are different, no matter how you turn them.

PoS 4/2d   **Understanding angle as a measurement of turn.**
PoS 4/2e   **Understand turning through right angles.**

Assessment in action

Ask children to get into pairs and take turns to play robots. Tell the 'instructor' to make the 'robot' move by saying 'half turn', 'quarter turn' and 'whole turn'. Hand signals would be helpful if the children want to use them to support their instructions.

Organisation
A hall would be ideal for this activity. It can be organised in the classroom, if you are only assessing two children, but it would probably be disruptive unless other children knew they would be able to 'have a turn' at another time.

Bilingual children may need more clarification and practise of the use of the terms. Signs or placards would be used. The child's home language should be used if this is normal practice in your class.

What might happen	*What this tells you*
1 Makes a turn, on the spot of approximately the number of right angles requested.	*Achieves the statements*, as the notion of a turn being an angle has been demonstrated by the physical turning of right angles.
2 Is not able to make the turns because of inadequate commands from the partner.	You may need to swap children around. Children who cannot use the terms may have language or confidence problems rather than a lack of understanding.
3 Turns inaccurately (eg through one right angle instead of two).	Turning right angles is difficult. If you believe the child does understand the turning of right angles, ask him/her how many right angles the big hand on the clock has turned. Observe him/her taking turns making the turtle turn right angles using Logo to give the child another context.
4 Is not completely accurate in the turns, but you believe understands right angles as he/she is a bright child.	Some children do not always perform a task to the best of their ability for its own sake. You may need to assess the child individually through a different context (eg drawing, map work).

Developing and extending understanding

- Using Logo, 'Pip' and 'Roamer' will help develop understanding through using angles and right angles.

- Children could play robots as described, first using the language 'quarter turn' and 'half turn'.

- Use the words 'right angle' when the *time* is discussed, to help children understand the concept of a quarter turn in various settings.

- Plot a treasure trail on a map of an island for someone else to solve, giving instructions for direction North, South, East and West and 90° turns.

- Give more complicated instructions for robot games (eg 45°, 90° turns).

- Use Logo to find out about other angles.

- Find how to make the turtle get as quickly as possible from one place to another with obstacles in the way. Keep a record of your programming. Look at your recording and see if there are any ways you could make the program shorter (eg FD 10, FD 10, FD 10 could be FD 30). 'Pip' or 'Roamer' may be easier to use for this task.

PoS 4/2f

Understanding the conservation of length, capacity and 'weight'.

About the statement

Conservation means understanding that the quantity of something stays the same, regardless of the way in which it is positioned or moved. (eg a length of string remains the same length no matter how the string is presented).

The difficulty with assessing children's understanding of conservation lies not so much with the concept as with the questioning. Changing the shape of something, then asking 'Is it still the same as it was?' (or similar), often leads to children assuming that the answer must be 'no', because of the leading nature of the question.

Assessment in action

This is best done informally and incidentally, when children are:

- measuring the length of something, using string;

- using a variety of containers to transfer water, sand, etc, from one to another;

- using Plasticine to make a given weight.

Length

Ask the child to cut the string the exact length of the object being measured and to find out how long it is. Then ask 'How long is the string?' (The answer does not have to be in standard units). Screw up the string and ask again 'How long is this string?' Finally, ask whether the length of the string stays the same or not when you screw it up.

Capacity

After the child has transferred the water/sand from one container to a different shaped container, ask 'Is there still the same amount of water/sand in this container as there was in that one?'

'Weight'

After the child has made a Plasticine weight, ask him/her to make it into an animal shape, and not to use any new Plasticine or take any away. Then ask if the animal weighs the same as it did before.

What might happen	*What this tells you*
Length	
1 Immediately tells you the same length, without measuring it again, and says that it makes no difference what shape the string is.	*Achieves the statement.* The child might look perplexed at your asking for the length a second time, but the final question should allow the child to explain. You could see how much more the child understands by asking what you would have to do to change the length of the string.
2 Tells you the same length, but then says that the length of the string changes when you screw it up.	The visual evidence often dominates a child's perception, so the word 'length' is forgotten. Ask the child more focused questions – eg 'What length was it?' (screw up the string), 'What length is it now?' (screw it up again), 'What length is it now?', etc. If the child does not see the link, ask him/her to measure the string again. You will need to assess the child again, because he/she should 'know' without finding out.
3 Gives a different length as answer to your second question.	Ask the child to measure the string again and repeat the procedure, continuing as above.
Capacity	
1 Tells you that the quantity is the same.	*Achieves the statement.* Find out the extent of the child's understanding by asking about the difference between the two containers. Also ask 'How do you know?' and 'What would you have to do to make the amount of water different?'
2 Tells you the second container holds either more or less.	The child could be confusing the total capacity of each container, which probably are different, rather than the actual amount of water which was transfered. Be more specific in your questioning, focusing on the *water* rather than the container.
Weight	
1 Tells you it weighs the same.	*Achieves the statement.* Find out more about the child's understanding by asking 'How do you know?' Ask how it could be changed.
2 Tells you it weighs more or less.	First check that the child did use exactly the same quantity first, or he/she could be right! Again, the child may be focusing on the appearance of the Plasticine, which probably now looks longer/taller, etc. Ask more specific questions about the actual Plasticine, maybe taking some yourself and changing its shape, as a demonstration.

Developing and extending understanding

Conservation tends to be grasped by children once they understand what is being asked of them and have had much practical experience. (See Piaget, Donaldson and Hughes for different accounts of children's ability to conserve – *Children's Minds*, by Margaret Donaldson (Fontana) provides a good summary.

The concept of conservation should be explored in a variety of mathematical situations. Collaborative tasks and sharing sessions provide an ideal setting for discussion of conservation. Focus on the idea of 'is it the same, more or less' with groups of children or the whole class. It will probably help children's understanding if the 'problems' are confronted (eg "I know it *looks* different, but let's forget how it looks – what do we already know about it?', etc.).

Ma 4

Ma 4/3a Sort shapes using mathematical criteria and give reasons.

Related PoS statement
- Sorting 2-D and 3-D shapes and giving reasons for each method of sorting. (PoS 4/3a)

About the SoA and related PoS statement

The use of mathematical criteria when sorting is emphasised in the SoA because of the wide variety of ways a collection of shapes could be sorted. Mathematical criteria might be by shape, size, number of edges/sides/corners, etc; ability to stack, roll, tessellate, etc. Non-mathematical criteria might include 'my favourite shapes', colour, material, etc.

The first part of the PoS statement is the same as level 1, except that re-sorting is now required. The second part ('giving reasons...') could be either oral or written, and would not need to be elaborate. The 'reason' is simply a statement of how the shapes have been sorted.

Assessment in action

Ask the child to re-sort the 2-D and 3-D shapes (see assessment for level 1a) and explain how the shapes have been sorted each time.

What might happen	*What this tells you*
1 Sorts in two different ways and gives reasons (ie tells you how they sorted.)	*Achieves the statement.*
2 Sorts in one way only, and cannot think of another way.	Is not yet able to 'start again' with the sorting, but can only see one way. The child needs to talk, with other children, about objects they are sorting (see extension ideas, below). Check level 1a.
3 Sorts, but cannot explain how he or she sorted.	Lacks the confidence and/or the necessary vocabulary. The child may need prompting (eg 'How are all these the same?', 'Why did you put all these shapes together?') and encouragement.

Developing and extending understanding

- Sorting in different ways is connected with the child's perception of the objects being sorted. If he/she has experienced lots of descriptive talk while exploring the objects, sorting follows much more naturally.

- Give children time to play with the objects before they are asked to sort them. Encourage exploration by saying (eg) 'Try to find out as much as you can about the ...'; 'Talk to each other about the ...'.

- Ask questions like 'Which one is your favourite?', 'Why do you like it?', 'Tell me about this one', 'What does this look/feel/smell/sound like?'.

- See also the extension ideas for PoS 4/1a, pages 75–6.

<table>
<tr><td>

Ma 4

</td><td>

Ma 4/3b   Recognise reflective symmetry.

Related PoS statement
● Recognising (reflective) symmetry in a variety of shapes in two and
  three dimensions. (PoS 4/3b)

</td></tr>
</table>

About the SoA and related PoS statement

The SoA is a broad statement which is defined in the PoS statement.

Recognising symmetry in 3-D shapes is difficult at this stage. It would be
advisable to give children experience of 3-D symmetry in the context of
exploring and cutting up Plasticine shapes. The following assessment is in two
parts: a resource sheet where children identify symmetrical shapes for the 2-D
reflection, and a sorting exercise and possible dialogue with the child for 3-D
reflection.

Assessment in action

Part 1   Give the child Resource Sheet 16 and explain the task.

Part 2   Ask the child to sort a collection of 3-D shapes and 3-D objects into
                            symmetrical and asymmetrical (or not symmetrical) sets.

                            Observe the sets and talk to the child if the shapes and objects have *not*
                            been correctly sorted. Ask the child to show you a shape which, if you cut it in
                            half, would produce one half and its reflection, or a mirror image, or similar
                            words.

                            Have a supply of tracing paper and mirrors for children to use if they want
                            to check the symmetry.

What might happen	*What this tells you*
Part 1	
1 Ticks at least five of the symmetrical shapes.	*Achieves the statement.* You could ask the child to draw in a line of symmetry, or as many lines as they can, for those shapes. This will enable you to see how much the child knows about lines of symmetry.
2 Ticks the asymmetrical shapes.	Talk to the child to find out whether he/she has simply reversed the terms.
3 Ticks both symmetrical and asymmetrical shapes.	The child does not have a clear enough understanding of symmetry. Ask him/her to draw in the mirror-lines, then see the extension ideas, below.
Part 2	
1 Sorts most of the shapes and objects appropriately.	*Achieves the statement.* Question the child about where you would need to 'cut' the shapes to make two symmetrical halves. This will inform you about how much the child knows about different lines of symmetry.

What might happen (cont)	*What this tells you*
2 The sorting seems unclear, but the child can explain where to 'cut' shapes to make symmetrical halves.	Ask him/her to sort them again after successfully explaining to you. The child may have misunderstood the task. If the sorting then proceeds, the child achieves the statement.
3 The sorting is unclear and the child is unable to explain the symmetry in 3-D shapes and objects.	Check that the task is completely understood. If the child still has difficulties, see the extension ideas, below.

Developing and extending understanding

- Listen to children discussing the tasks to gain insight into their perceptions.

- See Marion Walter's *Magic Mirror* books for a creative approach to learning about symmetry.

- Use small mirrors to change shapes and pictures and produce reflections of half-drawn pictures.

- Find lines of symmetry in 2-D drawings as well as 2-D shapes.

- Draw round 2-D shapes and cut them in half to check for symmetry.

- Play a pegboard symmetry game:

One player puts in a peg on his/her side of the board and the other player puts in the same colour peg on the other side to produce a symmetrical image. Build up a pattern in this way. Take turns being the 'creator':

etc

Change this to four areas, and produce two lines of symmetry: first player places one peg, second player completes all areas.

etc

- Make nets of 3-D shapes using straws and Plasticine (this will help children to see the 'inside' of a shape).

- Make 3-D shapes out of Plasticine (use pastry shape cutters and moulds) then cut in half to explore symmetry.

- Cut boxes in half in different ways to explore symmetry.

Ma 4

Ma 4/3c   Use the eight points of the compass to show direction.

Related PoS statement
- Using and understanding compass bearings and the terms 'clockwise' and 'anticlockwise'. (PoS 4/3c)

About the SoA and related PoS statement

The PoS statement extends the use of a compass to knowledge of 'clockwise' and 'anticlockwise'. Although it is easier for children to simply name the eight points of the compass, the SoA states that children should be able to *use* a compass as evidence of their understanding.

The assessment of 'clockwise' and 'anticlockwise' is best done incidentally, in conversation with a child, where there is a clear context. The following assessment reflects this approach.

Assessment in action

Part 1

Give each child being assessed Resource Sheet 17 and explain the task.

Part 2

Assess the child incidentally, by asking him/her to turn something clockwise or anticlockwise. If the child understands one of the terms, then you can assume this includes knowledge of the other term.

Ask the child what 'clockwise' or 'anticlockwise' means, or how he/she knew which way to turn it.

Any of the following contexts would lend themselves to an assessment: unscrewing a lid on a jar, turning a screw with a screwdriver, turning a door handle, turning a lever, turning a key in a lock, turning a clockwork key.

What might happen	*What this tells you*
Part 1	
1 Completes the map with various items drawn approximately in the correct areas.	*Achieves the statement.* The level of accuracy will tell you how well the child understands the concept of direction.
2 Draws some things in the correct place, but others are haphazard.	Talk to the child about the map, as he/she may have got 'carried away' by the context and forgotten to follow the instructions. Ask the child to point to the various regions of the map to check understanding – see extension ideas, below.
3 Draws all objects in the correct place, or cannot fit them all on.	Give the child a new map if he/she has run out of space, as children often draw their first things too big when they have been given a constricted space. If the drawings are still wrongly placed, the child either has difficulty with drawing or does not yet understand the meaning of compass points.

What might happen (cont)	*What this tells you*
Part 2	
1 Correctly turns an object either clockwise or anticlockwise and explains that the term is to do with the movement of clock hands.	*Achieves the statement.*
2 Hesitates before turning the object, in order to work out the direction, then turns the object appropriately and explains appropriately.	*Achieves the statement.* Most adults need this short pause to 'imagine' the movement of a clock before applying it.
3 Turns the object the wrong way, but explains correctly.	Give the child more and different opportunities to demonstrate achievement before you decide. If the child always reverses the terms, he/she may have simply confused the words but understands what 'clockwise' means.
4 Shows no consistency in turning one way or the other, and is unsure in explaining.	Needs practical experience of applying the understanding of 'clockwise'.

Developing and extending understanding

- Play 'North, South, East, West' in the hall, first showing children that you have checked where North is.

- Use compasses to find North, then point out the other directions, preferably in the context of a nature trail or something similar.

- Make up silly phrases to remember the compass points (eg 'Never eat shredded wheat', 'Naughty elephants squirt water').

- Make up treasure maps as in the Resource Sheet.

- Use a compass to plot out a route on a treasure map with directions for someone else to find the treasure (for very able children).

- Use the terminology 'clockwise' and 'anticlockwise' in the context of turning things in the classroom, and relate this to the movement of the hands of a clock.

- Play robots, using the terms 'clockwise' and 'anticlockwise' to describe the turns made.

- Link 'clockwise' and 'anticlockwise' with right and left in Logo.

Ma 5

Ma 5/1a Sort a set of objects, describing the criteria chosen.

Related PoS statements
- Selecting criteria for sorting a set of objects and applying them consistently. (PoS 5/1a)
- Recording with objects or drawing and commenting on the results. (PoS 5/1b)
- Creating simple mapping diagrams showing relationships and interpreting them. (PoS 5/1c)
- Recognising possible outcomes of random events. (PoS 5/1d)

About the SoA and related PoS statements

The SoA specifies only the first linking PoS statement. In terms of summative assessment, this is all the child would need to achieve. However, for your formative information, assessments of PoS 5/1b and 5/1c have been included.

PoS 5/1a

The use of the word 'select' in this statement implies that children should be making their own decisions about how to sort objects. The ability to 'apply consistently' is important, as it determines whether a child has actually sorted correctly or not. It would probably be acceptable for a child to have one object in the wrong set, although discussion often reveals the child's own logic for the inclusion.

PoS 5/1b

This statement is related to sorting. Recording with real objects could involve sticking them onto paper. The 'comment' could be oral or written.

PoS 5/1c

This statement is fairly complex and difficult, considering it is level 1. Children usually find *completing* mapping diagrams quite manageable, but *creating* a mapping diagram is obviously more difficult. The reading and interpretation of mapping diagrams is important because it is the main point of representing any data. It would be easier for children to read and interpret mapping diagrams which they have had some involvement in, or for which the context is clear.

PoS 5/1d

This statement appears not to link with the SoA, probably as a result of the redistribution of the 'old' AT14. It expresses something which most children do naturally: it seems unnecessary therefore to set up a situation to assess the statement when the behaviour can be observed fairly easily.

PoS 5/1a

Selecting criteria for sorting a set of objects and applying them consistently.

Assessment in action

This statement lends itself to incidental assessment, when children are already engaged in some kind of sorting. Good sorting collections include items such as buttons, lids, keys and coins, where there are many varieties of the same thing. The child should be asked to sort only one of these collections.

AT4 level 1a is a very similar assessment, except that shapes are used for sorting. If a child achieves this statement, you can assume that the above statement is also achieved. However, a child who does not achieve the statement when sorting shapes, may be able to achieve the above statement, as the context can be the sorting of any set of objects.

Observe the child sorting and ask how he/she sorted to make your assessment. If the child is sorting a collection of objects with other children, you will need to observe closely to make sure whether the child being assessed has chosen the sorting criterion.

What might happen	*What this tells you*
1 Sorts the objects consistently (ie keeps to the same rule and does not put objects in the wrong set). Tells you how the objects have been sorted.	*Achieves the PoS statement and the SoA.* Allow the child one or two misplaced objects at this stage.
2 Sorts the objects consistently, but is unable to tell you how they were sorted.	Achieves the PoS statement, but not the SoA. The child may have been influenced by other children's sorting, or may not have the language fluency to express the sorting. The child should still be offered sorting experiences even though the language is not yet developed. Paired sorting should encourage talk.
3 Cannot sort consistently, and tends to play with the objects or make pictures.	Children with particular difficulties might be over-stimulated by the objects. If you think this is the case, limit the sorting to one small collection (eg twenty buttons). See extension ideas, below.

Developing and extending understanding

- See extension ideas for PoS 4/1a, pages 75–6.

PoS 5/1b   **Recording with objects or drawing and commenting on the results.**

Assessment in action

This statement lends itself to assessment when children are recording any information regarding their sorting. Ask the child to show the information in some way on paper and tell you about it. Give this a purpose by explaining that this will show how they sorted even after the objects have been cleared away. Offer a choice of paper for recording.

What might happen	What this tells you
1 Records in some way, then comments about the recording, orally or in writing.	*Achieves the statement.* The comment should tell you how the child perceives the recording.
2 Records in some way, but provides no real comment.	Try to encourage the child to tell you something about the recording, by praising the work.
3 Records in some way, but the recording is not recognisable.	As long as the child can explain what it is, the statement can still be achieved. The child may have poor motor control, may have been slapdash, unmotivated, or perceives the object/people in a particular way. Discussion with the child should help determine which. All worthwhile efforts should be praised so that the child's confidence increases.

Developing and extending understanding

- Encourage the purpose of recording as early as possible, in ways which the child chooses.

- Make displays of objects, models, sets, etc, to show the value of 'recording'.

PoS 5/1c   **Creating simple mapping diagrams showing relationships and interpreting them.**

Assessment in action

First give the child Resource Sheet 18 to set the scene and remind him/her of what mapping means. Then, using a context which links with the class topic or a current focus, ask the child to collect some simple information and show it as a mapping diagram.

The following ideas may be useful: your table's/group's favourite colour (out of red, blue, yellow and green); way of getting to school; toys owned (from a given selection); pets owned; favourite fruits.

Talk to the child about the mapping diagram, asking him/her to explain it to you. You could use other children's mappings for the child to interpret. Ask questions like 'Does Darren like cabbage?'

What might happen	*What this tells you*
1 Completes the Resource Sheet and creates own mapping diagram successfully, and explains it to you.	*Achieves the statement.* Use the discussion with the child to see if he/she has any new ideas for developing the survey.
2 Completes the Resource Sheet, but it is not clear whether the child 'copied' someone else's mapping.	Children often use the same method as a group (eg all draw arrows). A child who really understands mapping is unlikely to be put on the wrong track by another child. However, a child who doesn't have a clear understanding will probably be unable to explain what he/she has done, or to complete a different mapping diagram on his/her own.
3 Creates own mapping diagram but continues to use the symbols used in the Resource Sheet.	The child probably lacks confidence in his/her own ability to use symbolic respresentation. This should develop as the child sees models of other kinds of mapping and is encouraged to make up his/her own.
4 Completes the Resource Sheet, but is unable to create own mapping diagram.	Creating a mapping diagram requires organisational skills, so the child may have collected the information but find reorganising it difficult (see extension ideas, below).
5 Is unable to understand and therefore complete the Resource Sheet.	The child needs to group real objects in a practical setting before going on to representation (eg sort toys, books, pictures, etc, into ones I like/ones I don't like).

Developing and extending understanding

- Use structured mapping diagrams to consolidate some practical experiments (eg objects which were/were not attracted to a magnet). This will enable children to see the style of mapping.

- Encourage group discussions about the creation of mapping diagrams.

- Encourage children to decide whether a mapping diagram is the most appropriate way of recording in each case. If there are too many lines, for instance, the diagram becomes illegible. Children could create their own ways of representing the data to make sure it is clear.

Ma 5

Ma 5/2a   Interpret relevant data which have been collected.

Related PoS statements
- Choosing criteria to sort and classify objects; recording results or outcomes of events. (PoS 5/2a)
- Designing a data collection sheet, collecting and recording data, leading to a frequency table. (PoS 5/2b)
- Constructing and interpreting frequency tables and block graphs for discrete data. (PoS 5/2c)
- Using diagrams to represent the result of classification using two different criteria, eg Venn and tree diagrams. (PoS 5/2d)

About the SoA and related PoS statements

Although the PoS statements are quite varied, the SoA states the main purpose of any data collecting: the *interpretation* of relevant data which have been collected. The PoS statements cover the range of types of data collecting which children need to engage in.

PoS 5/2a

The first part of this statement is the same as the SoA for level 1. The distinction between level 1 and level 2 is made by the second part, which requires the child to make some kind of *recording* of his/her sorting or the conclusions reached.

PoS 5/2b

A 'data collection sheet' can take any form, as long as it allows for collection of the relevant data. A 'frequency table' is a table of results based on the information collected. This does not have to include totals.

PoS 5/2c

The definition of a block graph often causes problems, as there are conflicting views about it, especially in relation to bar charts. However, SEAC guidance has stated that a block graph consists of a number of blocks, arranged vertically, where each block represents a single discrete item. The blocks could be coloured in squares or small drawings:

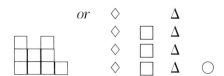

The labelling of the axes is not necessary for all block graphs, as long as their meaning is clear. The following would be acceptable:

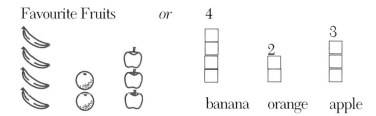

Block graphs are appropriate for representing data which deals with separate items – eg eye colour has to be recorded as separate, discrete colours, whereas height measurement, for instance, needs to be recorded on a continuous scale. The idea of 'interpreting' is important as it is the reason for constructing a graph in the first place, so there should not be *over*-emphasis on the construction of graphs. The graph should be seen as the starting point.

PoS 5/2d

There are other ways that sorting using two different criteria can be recorded, apart from Venn and tree diagrams – including, most importantly at this stage, children's own methods. It is important that children know the standard forms of diagramatic representation, but only when they are secure with their own ways or recording. The following assessment aims to find out whether children can record their sorting in a logical, clear way, It should be said, however, that this statement expects a high level of sophistication for children at this stage of development.

PoS 5/2a

Choosing criteria to sort and classify objects; recording results or outcomes of events.

Assessment in action

This statement lends itself to incidental assessment, when a child is sorting a collection of objects.

Choose a collection where the unit is the same, but varies from one to another (eg a collection of buttons or keys or lids). Children are often overwhelmed by variety, when a set of objects is too diverse. A collection of one unit (eg buttons) is more likely to encourage a child to sort according to different attributes (eg buttons with one, two or four holes, or by colour, shape, material, etc).

Ask the child to 'put something on paper to show someone how you sorted', giving the reason that the objects will have to be cleared away so they cannot be left for people to see.

If the child simply draws the sets, ask him/her to label them to show *how* he/she sorted.

What might happen	*What this tells you*
1 Writes a sentence or two to explain how he/she sorted (eg 'I put all the red buttons together, and all the blue buttons together ...' etc).	*Achieves the statement.* This form of recording could show the extent of sophistication the child has in sorting (eg if he/she wrote 'I sorted by colour' the child is generalising).
2 Draws a reproduction of the sorting, possibly by drawing round the objects, and labels the sets.	*Achieves the statement.* The child may feel that this is too time-consuming, in which case you could ask him/her how else the sets could be recorded. The child may enjoy drawing them, however.
3 Lays or sticks the objects onto the paper, with labels.	*Achieves the statement.*
4 Lays or sticks the objects onto the paper, without labels.	This is not a recording of results or outcomes. The labelling transforms it into something meaningful for the audience. Ask the child to show *how* the sets have been sorted to encourage him/her to achieve the statement.

Developing and extending understanding

- Encourage children to record their sorting and other practical work (eg modelling) in their own way, making the purpose clear (practical apparatus has to be cleared away, so we need a record). Recording something, if it is in the child's own way, helps consolidate mathematical thinking and often shows you the child's perception of what he/she has been involved in. This should not be done *every* time a child is involved in practical work, however, or he/she will find it tedious and time-consuming.

- Always have a variety of paper and card in different sizes for children to choose from, as this will affect how they record.

PoS 5/2b

Designing a data collection sheet, collecting and recording data, leading to a frequency table.

Assessment in action

Choose an area of interest which is linked with the class topic, for children to find out about. The following list of examples may be useful:

Food: which school dinner/vegetable/breakfast cereal, etc, is most popular?
Toys: which do most children want for Christmas/birthday?
Colour: which colour socks/tops/coats/trainers, etc, are most popular?
Shops: where do most people go shopping?
Transport: which colour car do more people drive in our street?
Class outing: where do most people want to go?
Class picnic: which sandwich fillings are most popular?

Ask children, in pairs, to design a sheet for collecting the information on. Observe this from time to time.

When the sheet is designed and discussed with you, ask the children to gather the information and show it clearly in a table of some kind.

Resources and organisation
Children will need a choice of paper for collecting information in their own way.

You may need to help pairs of children to organise themselves (eg one to collect information from half the class and one from the other half).

You should help children by asking questions rather than telling them, for example: 'How can you make the table clearer?', 'How do you know you've asked everyone in the class?', 'How could you check?'.

Be sensitive about ideas for collecting information – eg favourite cereal, when there may be children who are not given a breakfast; eye colour when all the children in the class are of Asian origin, etc).

What might happen	What this tells you
1 Participates in the design of the sheet, and then collects information and makes a table or chart.	*Achieves the statement.* Observe the extent of the child's dominance in the group, as this will tell you how much he/she understands about the elements of a data collection sheet (eg items, space for ticks or record, ordering, checking all collected).
2 Participates in the design of the sheet, but gets muddled when collecting the information.	Data collecting needs organisational and social skills, which the child may be unsure of. Watch how he/she asks children the survey question, as certain wording will not produce the required response (eg says 'Where do you want to go for the outing?' but forgets to state the six predetermined venues). The child needs simpler data collecting, such as 'Who has a cat and who has not?', for a Yes/No record, and needs to ask fewer people.

What might happen (cont)	*What this tells you*
3 Can help design the sheet and collect the information, but is confused by the making of a table or chart.	The child, having collected the information, cannot summarise it into a new form. He/she probably feels that there is no need for another list. Point out that (eg) it takes a long time for you to find all the people on his/her sheet who said they like chips because they are all spread out. This may prompt the child to regroup the data. However, data collecting is time-consuming and the child may be bored, so will need plenty of encouragement. A clear purpose (eg needing the chart to give someone who has asked for the information in an easy-to-read form) is more motivating.
4 Designs the data collection sheet so that it is already a table or chart, eg | Orange	1 1 1
Apple	1 1
Pear	1 1 1 1		*Achieves the statement.* You could ask the child to rearrange the data so that the items are ordered, and see whether he/she can convert this to a block or bar chart (PoS 5/2c).
5 Does not participate in the design of the sheet and finds the whole process difficult.	The child may be shy and might prefer to do this task alone.

Developing and extending understanding

- Begin data collecting as a class task, using a flip chart and pooling ideas. Starting points such as 'The school nurse needs to know who has had measles and who has not – how can we help her?' generate lots of suggestions for collecting and recording.

- To encourage and develop understanding, help children to design data collection sheets and maybe join in a group to give insecure children more confidence.

- The context must be very clear with data collecting, with an end-point obvious so that the child does not lose sight of the purpose of the task.

- It is helpful to have a pre-printed sheet of children's names available for data collecting. If children choose to record against their names, it can be extremely time-consuming and arduous for the names to be written out in the first place. However, these should be available only if that is how the children want to record.

- Collect similar information to compare to the original (eg 'Is red the favourite colour car in *all* the streets round here?', 'Do all the classes in the school prefer bananas to any other fruit?').

- Encourage children to question findings – '*Why* do most people shop at Tesco's?', '*Why* do most children want the latest fashion toy for Christmas?', etc.

- Children should follow up their own ideas for data collection wherever possible. Capitalise on children's questions, such as 'I wonder if everyone hates custard, like me?', by suggesting the child finds out.

PoS 5/2c

Constructing and interpreting frequency tables and block graphs for discrete data.

Assessment in action

This statement lends itself to incidental assessment, when a survey concerning discrete items is taking place (eg eye colour, hair colour, favourite animals, TV programmes, etc.)

Make sure children being assessed have had lots of experience of representing data in their own way, as well as being shown what a block graph is. A range of different sizes of squared paper should be available (large and small squares).

Ask the child to represent the data as a block graph, then tell you what he/she has found out.

What might happen

What this tells you

1 Draws a block graph and explains the main findings (eg 'Banana is the winner', 'The favourite fruit is banana').	*Achieves the statement.* See if the child can represent data as a bar chart (Ma 5/3b).
2 Represents the data in a form which is not a block graph (eg mapping, words picture, list).	Has not had experience of arranging data in the form of a block graph. This should be shown to a child as one of many ways to represent data.
3 Represents the data so it is *almost* a block graph (eg leaves out the labelling of the coloured blocks so that it is not clear what they represent).	Ask the child questions about the graph such as 'What do these blocks mean?' Encourage him/her to make the graph clearer without leading, so that you are not telling the child how to do it.

Developing and extending understanding

- Children should be encouraged from an early age to collect information and put it clearly on paper for someone to see their findings. If left to do this in their own ways, children usually start by drawing free pictures of the information. They then tend to arrange the pictures in sets. The next stage is usually the arrangement of the objects in lines, horizontally organised. This is not the way graphs are traditionally represented, so children need to be shown at this stage that we usually draw graphs in vertical arrays.

- Collecting information should be, if possible, at the instigation of the child, or spring from the child's curiosity so that the purpose is clear. There should always be something that is to be found out, rather than simply the construction of a graph for its own sake (eg if children are to collect information about which months their birthdays fall in, there should be a reason for this, so that subsequent interpretation of the data is meaningful). The survey should be able to lead on to further surveys in order to compare and draw inferences (eg do children in all the classes in the school dislike cabbage, or is it something only children of this age dislike? Is it the same for adults? Why do children seem not to like vegetables? How can we find out?).

PoS 5/2d   **Using diagrams to represent the result of classification using two different criteria, eg Venn and tree diagrams.**

Assessment in action

Ask the child to sort a collection of objects in two different ways. Discuss with the child which criteria the child could choose. (In trials, plastic letters were used and the child sorted into those with curved lines and those with straight lines.)

Try to find out what the child likes or is interested in about the objects, as this is more likely to lead to criteria which the child really understands – eg Ask what key he/she likes the best, from a collection of keys, and why. Thus, the first attribute might be 'shiny'. Ask what else he/she likes or finds interesting about the keys, until a different attribute emerges (eg 'gold', 'hole in the handle', etc).

After the child has sorted, talk to him/her about the sorting, making sure he/she understands what to do with things which belong in both sets or neither.

Explain that you would like the child to record the sorting in a diagram, so that someone else would know exactly where each object belonged in the sets. Say that the objects will have to be tidied away, which makes the purpose of the recording more clear.

Look at the child's diagram to assess the statement.

Resources and organisation

There should be a variety of collections of objects for children to choose from. You should also provide a variety of different types of paper for the child's recording.

The assessment does not require any special organisation, but it may prove time-consuming. You will therefore need to plan to assess a child when other children are occupied or you have additional classroom support. The assessment should be carried out when children are engaged in sorting, so that it is part of normal classroom behaviour.

What might happen	*What this tells you*
1 Records the sorting in a diagrammatic form which shows the objects in the correct place.	*Achieves the statement.* The important fact is that the objects should be in the correct place, whatever form the diagram takes. A child who records accurately shows a very high level of logical thinking.
2 Records the sorting so that not all objects are in the correct place (eg omits the objects which are not red or shiny).	It is common practice to 'forget' the objects which don't fit into the sets. The child needs to discuss the sorting with you (eg 'But where do these objects go? Do they still belong to the whole set of keys?' etc). The omission of the intersection in a Venn diagram is a lower level skill (see Ma5, levels 1a and 2a).
3 Does not sort the objects appropriately.	The child is probably not ready for sorting using two different criteria. Give the child lots of experience sorting with other children.

Developing and extending understanding

- It is best to encourage children to sort according to their own choice of attributes, which should emerge from their interest in the objects. If the sorting includes objects which belong in both sets and neither, you should capitalise on this as an opportunity to 'teach' the child the idea of a universal set. An intersection is best taught through the use of set rings, so that the merging of the sets happens as a physical act, preferably as a result of solving the problems of where to put the objects which fit in both sets.

- The choice of attributes, and the objects themselves, will determine, to a certain extent, how difficult the sorting will be. For instance, sorting into red buttons and blue buttons could result in three sets (red, blue and neither red or blue) or four sets (red, blue, neither or both), depending on the range of buttons.

- The recording of the sorting will be led, naturally, by the way in which the objects were arranged. Thus, it is much more likely that a child will record in a Venn diagram than a Carrol diagram.

- *What's in the Square?* is a commercially produced box of card matrices with accompanying picture cards, which progress in difficulty. It is a good way for children to become familiar with Carrol diagrams, as there is no drawing of charts or recording to be done. Instead the task is focused on the logical placing of the cards.

Ma 5

Ma 5/2b   Recognise that there is a degree of uncertainty about the outcome of some events but that others are either certain or impossible.

Related PoS statement
- Recognising that there is a degree of uncertainty about the outcomes of some events and that other events are either certain or impossible. (PoS 5/2e)

About the SoA and related PoS statement

The word 'recognise' in these statements is significant, as it implies that a child could only do this if he/she had experience of the context, and remembered or realised what was possible, probable or impossible. Children find it easier to be sure about possible and certain outcomes than impossible outcomes, probably because a child's world is full of seemingly possible impossibilities (in cartoons, comics and fantasy films, Father Christmas visiting every child in the world in one night, etc) when they are still learning about the world. Sophisticated children may also know enough about nuclear weapons, sudden death, etc., to know that even the most certain events (such as waking up tomorrow morning) may not in fact be absolutely certain.

The assessment of this SoA is difficult, therefore, because it is so dependent on the context and the interpretation the individual puts on certainty. The following assessment is built on a context which children should all have experienced, but you may need to modify this and decide how much a child understands through discussion.

Assessment in action

(This context is also used to assess level 3 (PoS 5/3e), so use it with children who achieve this assessment.)

After reading the class a story in which someone meets someone else as the central event, ask the children who they would meet if they walked all round the school. See if they can put at least one name under the categories 'certain', 'impossible', 'might'. Discussion will be a natural part of this process (eg 'You might meet your Mum in the school but I definitely won't meet mine because I know she's at work today').

What might happen	*What this tells you*
1 Is able to make at least one sensible suggestion of a person they might meet under each heading.	*Achieves the statement.*
2 Suggests people who do not seem appropriate under one or more headings.	Ask the child to explain the reason. It could be valid due to the circumstances or the child could give a good reason (eg 'I think the Queen might come to the school, because she sometimes visits children in school). If the child seems muddled, he/she has probably not enough experience of this particular context, or may have difficulty with the language involved in probability. Try using different words in discussing the chance.

Developing and extending understanding

- Involve children in the planning of 'real-life' situations, such as class visits, assemblies, projects, etc, where decision-making and discussion about likelihood arise naturally. In the planning of an outing, for instance, discussing which things *need* to be taken and which things *might* be needed would engage children in the decision-making process of deciding how important certain things would be. Any situation like this, where children have to decide on an order of preference or an order of necessity or similar, will help develop their skills of deciding probability. Practical activities and games, where there is no debate about the meaning of terms, may make it easier for children to understand the mathematical principles of probability, for example:

  - board games where there are different routes, including routes that must be taken, might be taken, or were not taken.
  - predicting outcomes for filling containers to see which ones will overflow or not; similarly, for weight, objects which will go over a certain weight, etc.

  Discussion of such experiences will be essential for children to draw their own conclusions about likelihood.

Ma 5/3a   Access information in a simple database.

Related PoS statements
- Extracting specific pieces of information from tables and lists. (PoS 5/3a)
- Entering and accessing information in a simple database, eg card database. (PoS 5/3b)
- Entering data into a simple computer database and using it to find answers to simple questions. (PoS 5/3c)

About the SoA and related PoS statements

The SoA implies that 'access' should involve entering and extracting information, although if the SoA is taken literally, a child will achieve it by extracting information from any given table, list or computer database.

PoS 5/3a

The purpose in making a table or a list is to allow easy access to the information it presents. This statement is linked with the activity for PoS 5/2b because children will have made a table or chart which can be used to facilitate the assessment. Children are much more likely to be able to achieve this statement if the table or list is one they have been involved in in some way, rather than one which has been made by someone else and is 'out of context'.

PoS 5/3b

This statement refers to *any* database, whether a computer is involved or not. Therefore, this assessment focuses on a classroom database.

PoS 5/3c

Two programs which are suitable for assessment of this statement are *Our facts* and *Clipboard*. Details are given in the reference section. The 'answers to simple questions' may arise from the child's or teacher's questions. The assessment of this statement depends entirely on use and experience of the software. It is not appropriate, therefore, to include a separate activity here.

PoS 5/3a   **Extracting specific pieces of information from tables and lists.**

Assessment in action

Use the assessment activity on page 111 (PoS 5/2b) as a starting point.

Once the data is collected and recorded, ask the children being assessed to tell you *two* specific facts from the table (eg 'Tell me which car colour is most/least popular'). You could ask other children to explain their findings, possibly at sharing time, so that extracting information is emphasised and valued.

What might happen	*What this tells you*
1 Extracts information from the table, in answer to your questions.	*Achieves the statement.* Ask how he/she looked for the information, as this could give you useful insights into his/her strategies.
2 Cannot extract the relevant information from the table.	You need to be sure that the child understands your question. Change the question to 'tell me something that this table tells you' or similar. You will probably know how far the child was involved in the design of the sheet and collection of data, which may point to reasons for the lack of success. At another time, try to encourage the child to work with someone very supportive.

Developing and extending understanding

- See the extension ideas for PoS 5/2b, page 112.

PoS 5/3b

Entering and accessing information in a simple database, eg card database.

Assessment in action

Make, with the children, a classroom graph or table of facts which will be interesting to the children and which is ongoing, for example:

- a daily record of the weather;
- a daily record of the temperature;
- a monthly record of children's heights;
- a weekly record of money collected for a particular charity.

The making of the 'database' should be collaborative, with the children's ideas being reinforced, discussed and taken up by you.

In sharing times, or during the day, ask children whom you choose to assess for this statement, to enter the new information and then tell you something about the record so far, eg 'What was the weather like last Tuesday?'

What might happen	*What this tells you*
1 Is able to enter information into the class database, and tells you something specific about it.	*Achieves the statement.* Look for evidence of the child showing more than the statement, eg making a prediction about what will happen next/generalising about the information/making a hypothesis (eg 'Whenever it is ... we always get' ...).
2 Can enter information but finds it difficult to extract it.	Entering information is easier as it is the last record made, whereas finding information involves looking back and searching for a particular day. The child needs to be involved in group discussions where information is extracted.
3 Finds it difficult to enter or extract information.	Probably does not understand the purpose of the database and/or is not at this stage. Check that the child understands the database.

Developing and extending understanding

- Context is all-important when working with a database. The child needs to know what the database is for, how the information is recorded, what form the recording takes and how the whole database is designed so that past records can be found.

- Start with 'easy' contexts, like the class weather record. This is ideal for entering and extracting information.

- Encourage children to talk together and to you about the database, and ask questions to provoke a prediction (eg 'Looking at how much you've grown so far, how much do you think you'll grow in the next month?').

- Use computer databases, such as *Our Facts.*

- Encourage comparison of data and some kind of analysis (eg 'Is there a pattern of results for every Wednesday?').

- Encourage children to use and make databases to link with class topics (eg birds seen today). Once a certain amount of information is collected, it can be analysed and discussed.

Ma 5/3b   Construct and interpret statistical diagrams.

Related PoS statement
- Constructing and interpreting bar charts and graphs (pictograms) where the symbol represents a group of units. (PoS 5/3d)

About the SoA and related PoS statement

The SoA uses the broad term 'statistical diagrams' which is then defined in the PoS statement as 'bar charts' and 'pictograms'. The definitions and assessment activities which follow deal with these separately.

Bar charts

The definition of a bar chart often causes problems, especially as a block graph and bar chart have been perceived as important ways for children to record, yet the difference between them is often muddled.

SEAC guidance has stated that a **block graph** is used for individual blocks, as in the collection of discrete data, where the answer can only be represented in whole numbers or blocks. A **bar chart**, however, deals with continuous bars, with a continuous scale. A survey of height measures, for instance, would be best represented as a bar chart, where the scale divides into fractions.

The labelling of the vertical axis is necessary in a bar chart, and it is important that the *lines* are numbered rather than the spaces, to ensure that the squares are not perceived as individual units. The labelling of zero is not vital, as long as a space has been left for it.

The following examples of bar charts are acceptable:

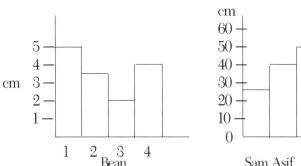
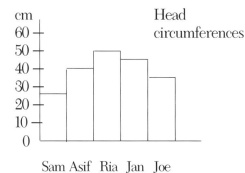

The focus of a bar chart, or any recording of data, should be on what can be interpreted from it, rather than on its construction for its own sake. The following assessment reflects this view.

Reading a graph is simply describing it (eg 'There are six more boys than girls') whereas *interpreting* is about drawing conclusions (eg 'It shows that red is the most popular car colour'/'Not many men go shopping in the daytime'). The next stage – not included in this assessment – would be to ask the child *why* he/she thinks this is so.

Pictograms

This attribute refers to the kind of pictogram which is most often used by the media, where a symbol represents a thousand people or a family for instance. The purpose of these graphs is to be visually explicit and simple, so that complicated scales do not have to be digested. However, children rarely collect so much evidence that there is a need for the use of such symbols, and they usually use a scaled axis (eg 0, 10, 20, 30, etc) when large amounts are involved.

The symbol may need to be halved or quartered to show any remainders. This cannot be drawn accurately, but the drawing should approximate the fraction (eg half a car/half a person).

An example of a pictogram using symbols to represent a group of units is as follows:

Favourite fruit

Mango	☺ ☺ ☺ ◖
Apple	☺ ☺
Pear	☺ ☺ ◗
Banana	☺

☺ = 10 children

The following assessment aims to set up a situation where children are asked to use symbols, with the emphasis focused on their ability to interpret and construct the pictogram.

PoS 5/3d(i)   **Constructing and interpreting bar charts**

Assessment in action

This attribute lends itself to assessment when a survey concerning continuous measures is taking place (eg height measure, head circumference, weights of different parcels, etc). This assessment need not be in the context of a 'mathematics' session, as surveys are often carried out in the context of a science or language based activity.

Children should have had lots of experience of representing data from surveys in their own way, as well as being shown how to construct a bar chart at some time. It would be unwise to 'teach' how to construct a bar chart at the same time as you intend to assess a child's knowledge and understanding of it: it would be better to assess this SoA when you believe a child has had sufficient experience of constructing and interpreting bar charts and you would like to confirm his/her achievement. A range of different sizes of squared paper should be available (large and small squares).

Ask the child to make a bar chart to show the information, then tell you what he/she has found out. Alternatively, ask the child to interpret someone else's graph ('What is shown on this graph? So why do you think that is?').

What might happen

1 Draws a bar chart and explains the main findings (eg 'The boys seem to have the biggest heads', 'Razia is the shortest, but she is the youngest').

2 Represents the data in a form which is not a bar chart (eg mapping, words, pictures, lists, block graph).

What this tells you

Achieves the attribute. Discuss the use of scales if you believe the child has had to use large sheets of paper in order to fit on the vertical scale – talk about different ways the numbers could be written to use less paper.

Needs more experience of arranging data in the form of a bar chart. If the child's recording shows the data clearly it should be valued: it simply does not meet the criteria to enable you to assess this attribute.

Developing and extending understanding

● Children should be encouraged from an early age to collect information and 'show it clearly on paper' for someone else to see what they have found out. If left to do this in their own ways, children usually start by drawing free pictures of the information. They then tend to arrange the pictures in sets.

The next stage is usually the arrangement of the objects in lines, horizontally organised. This is not the way graphs are traditionally represented, so children need to be shown, at this stage, that we usually draw graphs in vertical lines. Collecting information should be, wherever possible, at the instigation of the child, or spring from the child's curiosity, so that the purpose is clear. Many situations arise, in the context of cross-curricular activities and from 'real-life' situations, where information needs to be collected. There should always be something definite which is to be found out, rather than the meaningless construction of graphs for their own sake (eg If children's head circumferences are to be collected, there should be a reason for this, such as seeing whether there is a difference between girls' and boys' heads or for finding out how much card we need to make hats.) The purpose usually dictates the most appropriate recording form for the data. In the previous example, a bar chart would be inappropriate, for instance displaying the head circumferences so that they could be added up easily to see how much card was needed.

- Surveys should be able to lead on to further surveys in order to compare and draw worthwhile inferences (eg Is there a difference between boys' and girls' head circumference in every class in the school, or is it something to do with age? How do adults' heads compare to children's? How many adults would we need to use to find out? How about babies' heads? Is head size hereditary or related to any other part of the body?, etc).

PoS 5/3d(ii)   **Constructing and interpreting graphs (pictograms).**

Assessment in action

Children who are to be assessed for this attribute should have had experience of using symbols in pictograms, or at least, interpreting them. It would be unwise to use this experience for assessment if it is the first time a child has used symbols in this way.

Linking to the context of a class topic or relevant focus, ask children to find out either

- *Which colours of cars are most popular?*, or
- *How many men/women go into a local supermarket at a certain time?* (in order to draw conclusions about shopping habits/gender issues/compare with other times of the day, etc).

Have a group/class discussion about what might happen. Encourage children to predict findings and say *why* this might be. This will not only motivate the children, but will help them to formulate opinions for interpreting the data.

The survey will need to involve large numbers, so use a main road for the traffic count, and a supermarket rather than a small shop for the shopping count.

Once the information has been collected, ask the children to make a pictogram, using a symbol, such as one car to represent ten cars, or one woman to represent ten women. Give these as examples and encourage children to devise their own symbols, to represent as many cars/people as they think is sensible.

Decide on the extent of the child's achievement after the pictogram has been constructed and interpreted, depending on how much you have had to 'teach' him/her how to do it.

When the graph is finished ask the child to explain how many cars/people are in each column and to give some kind of opinion for the possible reasons for the findings.

Resources and organisation

You will, of course, need to plan to do this when you can use another adult for escorting children off the school premises.

Children can work cooperatively in the collecting of the information, although each child will need his/her own information in order to create a pictogram. The method of collecting the information could be decided cooperatively by the children, but the pictogram should be done by each child individually, so that you can make a reliable assessment.

Children should be provided with a range of paper, etc, so that they can choose their own ways of collecting and representing the information.

What might happen	*What this tells you*
1 Creates a pictogram using symbols, describes it correctly and gives an opinion which shows an attempt to draw inferences from the data (eg 'I think there were more red cars because more people like the colour red, as it is cheerful', 'Most of the men and women shopping together were old, so I think they are probably retired').	*Achieves the attribute.* Look for correct use of splitting the symbol for any remainders, as this will show the child's understanding of fractions. (It does not need to be accurate for this statement.) Also look for the appropriateness of the number the symbol represents (eg one car representing 20 cars when only 23 were counted is inappropriate, although the attribute is still achieved). Encourage the child to follow up the findings (see extension ideas, below).
2 Creates a pictogram and explains it, but gives no opinion about the results.	Offer suggestions of reasons for the findings, then ask the child if he/she can think of any other reasons. This should help the child to see the point of the task.
3 Has difficulty in creating a pictogram, perhaps using different symbols rather than the same one, or mixing up what each symbol is worth.	Discuss the pictogram with the child, asking him/her to explain what the columns mean and helping him/her to see how it might confuse someone trying to interpret it. Have a sharing session where some children show and explain their pictograms, as this will most sensitively help the child to understand the use of symbols without undermining his/her confidence.

Developing and extending understanding

- See the other references to collecting, recording and interpreting data at levels 1 and 2.

- Make sure that there is a clear purpose in collecting large numbers, as the collecting can be time-consuming, and will demotivate children if it seems pointless. The purpose will also clearly affect the appropriateness of the recording and any inferences to be made.

- Also make sure that the information is not being collected in this way just to create a pictogram, when there may be a more sensible way of finding out the information. For example, finding out how many children stay to school dinner is best done by looking at the dinner registers rather than counting all the children. Children should come to this conclusion themselves, of course, through discussion with you and each other in deciding how to collect the data.

- The exercise will become more meaningful and provide richer learning experiences for the children if the findings are followed up in some way (eg Is it only on this street that red cars are the most popular? Is it true for other vehicles as well? Could it be because more red cars are produced than other colours? How could we find out? etc).

- Help children to learn how to represent the data by modelling it, using eg Dienes cubes and sticks (ten units represented by one stick). This will smoothen the link to creating a pictogram.

Ma 5/3c   Use appropriate language to justify decisions when placing events in order of 'likelihood'.

Related PoS statements
- Placing events in order of 'likelihood' and using appropriate words to identify the chance. (PoS 5/3e)
- Understanding and using the idea of 'evens' and saying whether events are more or less likely than this. (PoS 5/3f)
- Distinguishing between 'fair' and 'unfair'. (PoS 5/3g)

About the SoA and related PoS statements

In order to achieve the SoA a child would only need to achieve the first PoS statement. Assessment activities have been included for the other PoS statements, however, for your formative information about a child's progress.

PoS 5/3e

This statement takes the corresponding level 2 statement (PoS 5/2e) on to ordering the events according to how likely they are to happen. 'Likelihood' is in quotes because this depends entirely on the circumstances and therefore cannot be deemed to be right or wrong. The 'appropriate words to identify the chance' would be statements like 'more likely', 'very unlikely', etc.

Trials proved this assessment to be very successful with bilingual children, and focused their attention on the words used for probability. However, you may need to use an interpreter or spend extra time making the terms clear.

PoS 5/3f

'Evens' is the term for there being an equal chance of something happening (eg there is an even chance of a coin landing heads facing up). The following assessment aims to put this concept in a simple form.

PoS 5/3g

Children find it difficult, at this stage, to differentiate between fairness as justness related to them personally and mathematical or scientific fairness. The idea of *un*fairness seems more readily to prompt fairness, so the following assessment aims to start from an 'unfair' situation.

PoS 5/3e

Placing events in order of 'likelihood' and using appropriate words to identify the chance.

Assessment in action

This assessment activity links with the activity for PoS 5/2e, in which children are asked to discuss who they might meet if they walked around the school, and categorise these into 'certain', 'impossible' or 'might happen'.

Ask children who achieved the level 2 task to put some of the ideas children had in order, on a probability line, as there may be some people who, for instance, you are more likely to meet than others, etc.

Encourage children to do this in their own way. This may mean writing down the suggestions and physically ordering them, or just talking to you about the names already listed and ordering them verbally.

This assessment can be organised in a variety of ways, depending on how many children you wish to assess. However, it may prove difficult to find out what every child has to say if the group is too large.

The probability line should show a continuum:

Definitely won't meet ... Might meet ... Definitely will meet

What might happen	*What this tells you*
1 Is able to order people you might meet, according to the likelihood.	*Achieves the statement.* The discussion with the child about the reasons for the ordering should reveal more about his/her knowledge of the world and the school than of maths. Debating the probability of meeting someone in the school will enable the child to display his/her maturity and reasoning ability better than many other oral exchanges in school.
2 Is not able to order the people you might meet.	Is probably not at the level of sophistication to differentiate the likelihood. This may be a language difficulty rather than a lack of perception. Discussion with the child should help to clarify this.

Developing and extending understanding

- See the extension ideas for PoS 5/2e, page 117.

PoS 5/3f   **Understanding and using the idea of 'evens' and saying whether events are more or less likely than this.**

Assessment in action

Preferably within the context of an investigation using cubes or of a probability experiment, ask the child being assessed to place red and blue cubes in a bag so that there would be an even chance of taking out a cube of either colour.

If the child does this successfully (ie puts an equal number of red and blue cubes in the bag, or tells you that you would need to put an equal number in), ask him/her what you would have to put in the bag to be more likely to take out a red cube. The child may wish to do this practically rather than tell you.

What might happen	*What this tells you*
1 Tells you or shows that an equal number of each colour would need to be placed in the bag, and says that there would need to be more red cubes than blue for the red to be more likely.	*Achieves the statement.* Ask the child how many more red cubes than blue cubes there would need to be for the red to be more likely. If he/she says one more, the child is showing a high level of logical ability and understanding of probability.
2 Is able to explain evens but finds difficulty with the second part of the task.	Make sure the child is given the chance to use the cubes to find out. If he/she still has difficulties, give the child the opportunity to experiment with a partner, using only a few cubes at a time and recording each cube's colour as it is taken out.
3 Is unable to explain or show the idea of evens.	Make sure the child understands the question. Do not go on to the second part of the task (see extension ideas, below).

Developing and extending understanding

- Give children lots of practical experiences of finding what is needed to have an even chance, for example:

  - to get red on a two-coloured die;
  - to pick a girl out of a group of children;
  - to have a coin land heads up;
  - to throw a six on a die.

- Once the concept of evens is established, the idea of being more or less likely tends to follow more naturally, as the distortion of one of the factors has a strong visual impact (eg to make it more likely to get a six on a die by numbering the die with more sixes than other numbers, is somehow clearer than there being an equal chance of getting a six, or any other number, when there is only one of each number on the die.)

PoS 5/3g   **Distinguishing between 'fair' and 'unfair'.**

Assessment in action

During the playing of a game involving a board, cards, dice, etc, discuss how the game could be changed in some way so that it was *unfair*. You could suggest that one thing (eg the dice) could perhaps be altered, or maybe one of the rules of the game.

After something has been suggested, ask what you would need to do to make the game *fair*, so that there is the same chance of winning for all players.

What might happen	*What this tells you*
1 Suggests an unfair strategy (eg allowing one player to have two throws of the dice) then says what would be fair (eg allowing each player one throw of the dice).	*Achieves the statement.* The important factor is that the conditions should be the same for all players.
2 Says something inappropriate (eg 'Don't let Sam play').	The child needs to be directed to the rules of the game. By playing a game with unfair rules, he/she is more likely to develop understanding.

Developing and extending understanding

- An excellent way of developing an understanding of fairness is for children to create their own games. If the games are played and analysed to see how well they work, the concept tends to occur naturally.

- Group discussions in the playing of games will also extend children's thinking. Ask children how a game can be changed in some way as an extension activity, to get the most out of games. Suggest that one thing should be changed at a time (eg the numbers on the die, the number of dice used, the rule applied to how one moves along the track, etc) and the game tried again to see how well it works.

- Science experiments lend themselves to the idea of fairness. In testing the strength of two magnets, for example, it would be a fair test if both magnets picked up the same things (eg paper clips of the same size). In comparing rates of growth of two plants, all conditions would have to be the same (eg light, water, soil) in order for the test to be fair.

RESOURCE SHEETS

(photocopy masters)

Published by Hodder & Stoughton
The publishers grant permission for copies of this sheet to be made in the place of purchase for use solely in that institution.

Formative Assessment in the National Curriculum: Mathematics

RESOURCE SHEET I

Published by Hodder & Stoughton. The publishers grant permission for copies of this sheet to be made in the place of purchase for use solely in that institution.

Published by Hodder & Stoughton
The publishers grant permission for copies of this sheet to be made in the place of purchase for use solely in that institution.

Formative Assessment in the National Curriculum: Mathematics

RESOURCE SHEET 3

8 8 3 2 3 7 5 3 7 0 5 6 1

Talk about FRACTIONS

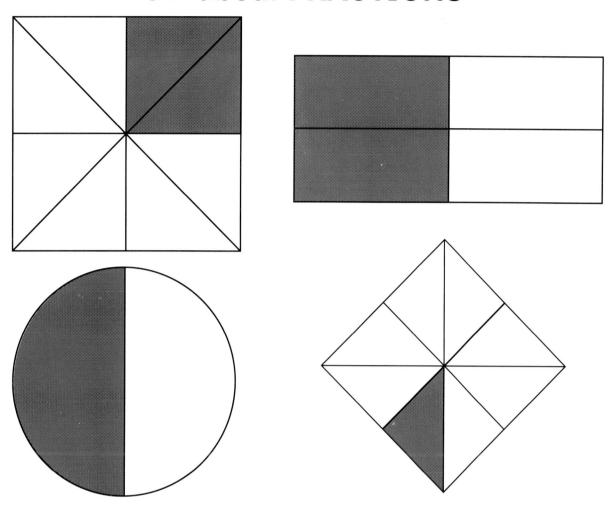

How many different ways can you colour in **HALF** of each big square?

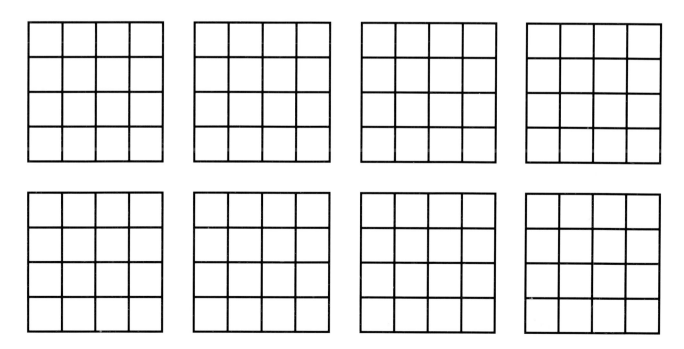

585 | 55 | 1 | 79 | 1 | 270 | 32 | 55 | 53 | 95 | 1 | 7

✂

14	18	16
12	15	17
14	13	15
13	18	15
15	14	16
16	13	17

Published by Hodder & Stoughton.

16	10	13 [−]
13	12	14
14	11	15
13	17	14
15	14	16
15	11	12 [−]

TABLE FACTS

Join each table fact to its answer. The first one has been done for you.

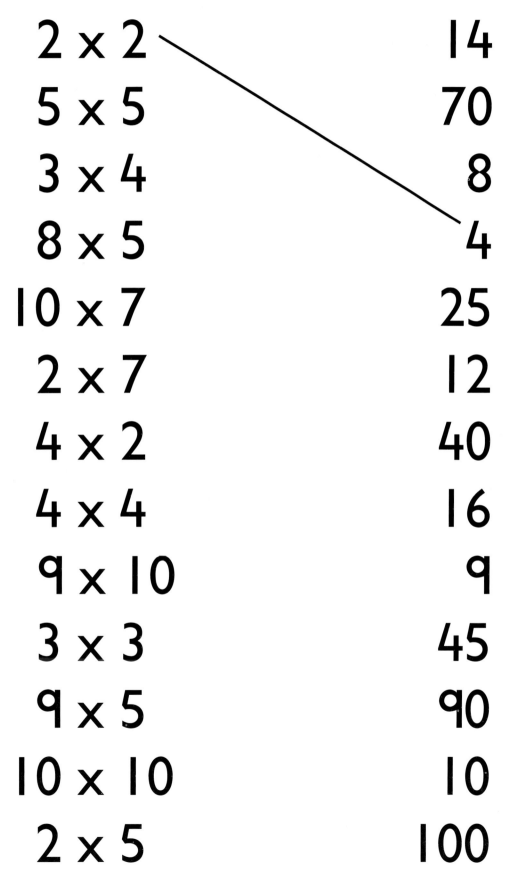

2 x 2	14
5 x 5	70
3 x 4	8
8 x 5	4
10 x 7	25
2 x 7	12
4 x 2	40
4 x 4	16
9 x 10	9
3 x 3	45
9 x 5	90
10 x 10	10
2 x 5	100

ROUNDING UP AND ORDERING

Write these numbers **in order**

| 465 | 231 | 599 | 604 | 910 | 747 | 123 |

| | | | | | | |

Round these numbers to the nearest **10**

37 ➔ ☐   92 ➔ ☐

22 ➔ ☐   28 ➔ ☐

45 ➔ ☐   69 ➔ ☐

Round these numbers to the nearest **100**

275 ☐   450 ☐   899 ☐

320 ☐   105 ☐   646 ☐

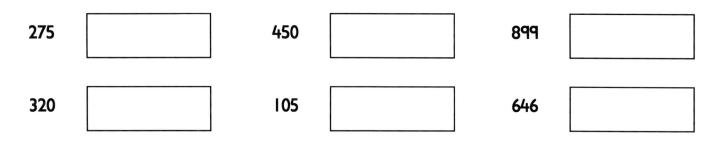

Published by Hodder & Stoughton.   The publishers grant permission for copies of this sheet to be made in the place of purchase for use solely in that institution.

9 3

30 10

6 5

24 11

1

7 11

12

16

3

Published by Hodder & Stoughton
The publishers grant permission for copies of this sheet to be made in the place of purchase for use solely in that institution.

Formative Assessment in the National Curriculum: Mathematics
RESOURCE SHEET 9

SYMBOLS

1. Fill in the gaps

1, 2,   , 4, 5, 6,   , 8

2. What does the symbol ✱ stand for?

3. What **could** these symbols stand for?

→

→

→

→

Published by Hodder & Stoughton.

NUMBER PATTERNS

Complete these number patterns

1. | 2 | 4 | 6 | 8 | | | | | |

2. | 0 | 5 | 10 | 15 | | | | | |

3. | 0 | 10 | 20 | 30 | 40 | | | | |

4. | 0 | 15 | 25 | 35 | 45 | | | | |

Make up some patterns of your own for a friend to complete

5.

6.

7.

8.

9.

Published by Hodder & Stoughton.

DIVIDING BY 2, 5 AND 10

Join the numbers to the correct circle (or circles).

The first one has been done for you.

REMEMBER – some numbers might join to more than one circle.

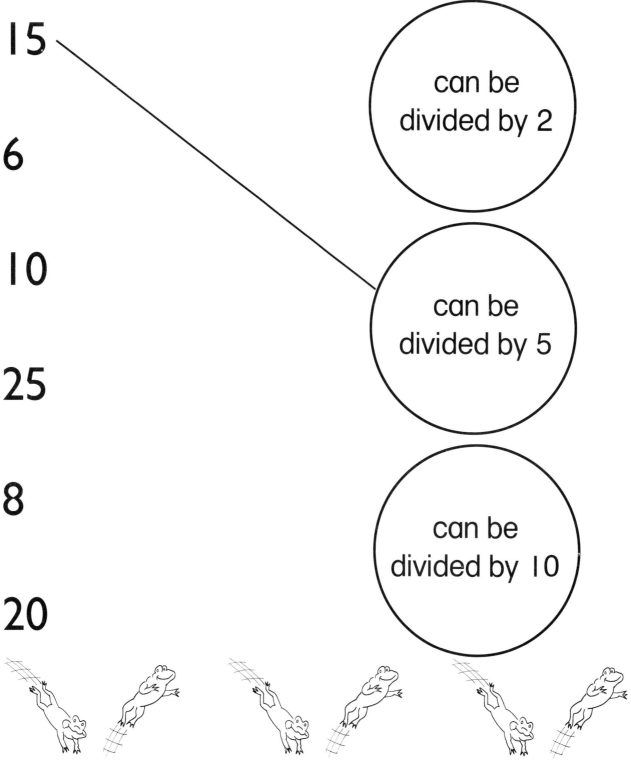

15

6

10

25

8

20

can be divided by 2

can be divided by 5

can be divided by 10

Published by Hodder & Stoughton.

Fill in the gaps. Show what happens once the machine has changed the input.

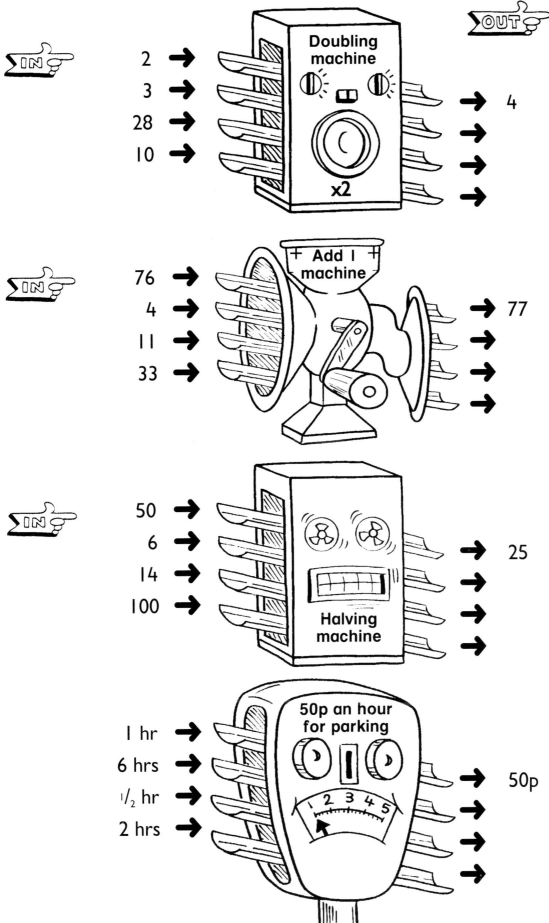

The publishers grant permission for copies of this sheet to be made in the place of purchase for use solely in that institution.

Find the hidden shapes in the picture. Then colour them in using the colour key.

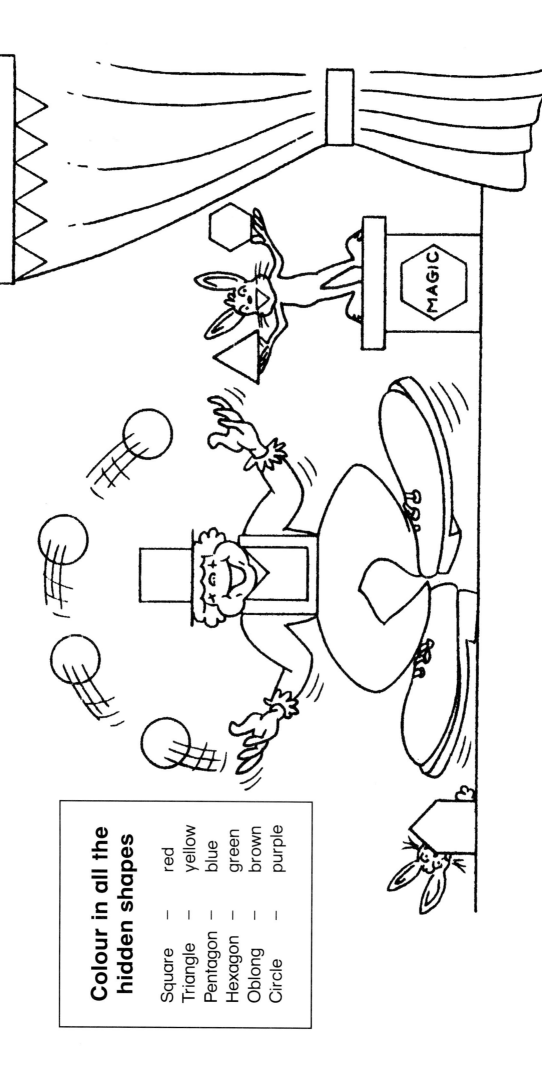

Colour in all the hidden shapes

Square	– red
Triangle	– yellow
Pentagon	– blue
Hexagon	– green
Oblong	– brown
Circle	– purple

MAGIC

Published by Hodder & Stoughton
The publishers grant permission for copies of this sheet to be made in the place of purchase for use solely in that institution.

Formative Assessment in the National Curriculum: Mathematics
RESOURCE SHEET 14

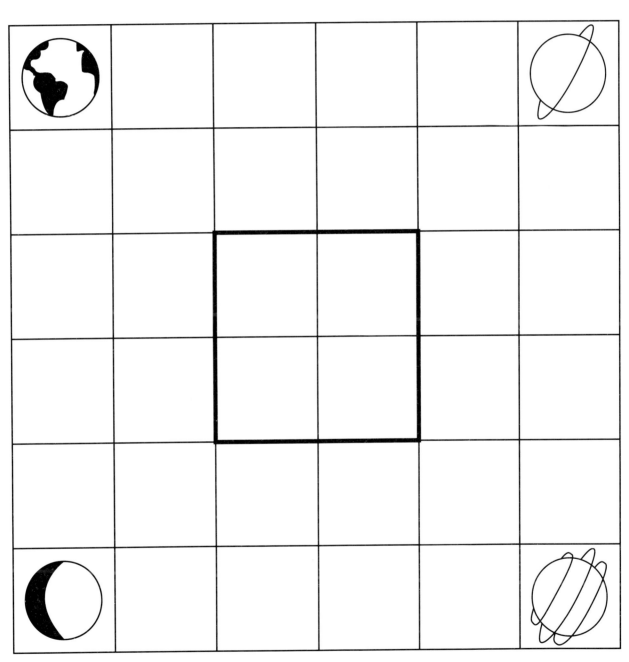

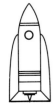  Cut out to use as counters

Published by Hodder & Stoughton.

SYMMETRY

Tick **only** the shapes which are **symmetrical**

TREASURE MAP

Draw these onto the map, in the right place

1. A tree at N.

2. You in the E.

3. Mountains in the NE.

4. A lake in the S.

5. A buried treasure sign at SW.

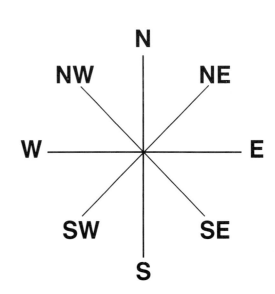

Draw lines to show what food you **like** and **don't like.**

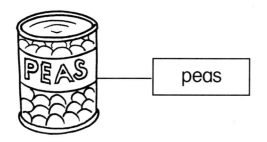

peas

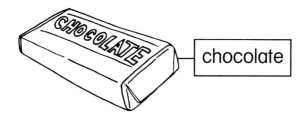

chocolate

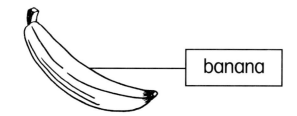

banana

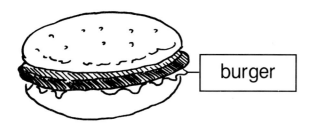

burger

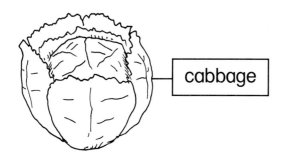

cabbage

I like

I **don't** like